Oh, La La!

Oh, La La!

Homegrown Stories, Helpful Tips, and Garden Wisdom

CISCOE MORRIS

SASQUATCH BOOKS

SEATTLE

Printed in the United States of America

SASQUATCH BOOKS with colophon is a registered trademark of Penguin Random House LLC

24 23 22 21 20   9 8 7 6 5 4 3 2 1

Editor: Susan Roxborough
Production editor: Jill Saginario
Designer: Tony Ong
Cover photographer: Charity Burggraaf

Library of Congress Cataloging-in-Publication Data
Names: Morris, Ciscoe, author.
Title: Oh, la la! : homegrown stories, helpful tips, and garden wisdom / Ciscoe
   Morris.
Description: Seattle, WA : Sasquatch Books, 2020. |
Identifiers: LCCN 2019020436 | ISBN 9781632172792 (paperback) | ISBN
   9781632172808 (ebook)
Subjects: LCSH: Gardening--Anecdotes.
Classification: LCC SB318.3 .M67 2020 | DDC 635--dc23
LC record available at https://lccn.loc.gov/2019020436

ISBN: 978-1-63217-279-2

Sasquatch Books
1904 Third Avenue, Suite 710
Seattle, WA 98101

SasquatchBooks.com

To the four survivors, the best storytellers I know

Contents

INTRODUCTION

I am a storyteller. My mom and dad were a professional dance team that performed in vaudeville throughout the Midwest and East Coast. It's no surprise that they regaled their seven children with stories at the dinner table each evening. Not only did I become a storyteller, my six siblings did as well. Dinner at our house was total pandemonium with everyone competing to tell the best story.

The stories in this book come from my long and varied career in gardening, media, world travel, and life in general. I've worked for private garden companies, big and small. I have run my own garden business, and I directed the grounds care at Seattle University for twenty-four years. Many of my garden stories (a.k.a. misadventures) take place at Seattle University and at my home, much to the chagrin of my wife. Insects play a key role (both good and bad) in the garden, so they take center stage here as well. My passion for dogs and travel intertwines with gardening, which has led to many zany adventures along life's path. And how could I write a book without including my much-beloved brussels sprouts?

I regularly speak in front of live audiences. My talks are focused on some aspect of gardening, but I always manage to finagle in a few stories. Often, a fan will shout out "Tell the Oh, La La story" or request some other tale. My stories might not always relate directly to gardening, but they definitely shed some light on my crazy character.

Oh, La La!

PART 1

Pruning and Haircuts

The Rule of Pruning and Haircuts: Know When to Stop

Pruning is a bit like cutting hair: it is an art form that helps both humans and plants look their best, but you don't want to overdo it. Before I go into pruning, let me focus on haircuts so I can share one of my all-time favorite stories and let you know more about me. Don't worry: you'll find plenty of garden tips in the book.

As a young kid, growing up in the '50s, my best friend's father, Mr. Eirman, was the free "barber" for our family. Once a month, my brothers and I were subjected to "haircuts" from Mr. Eirman. They actually were not haircuts at all—rather, he lined us up and shaved our heads. I didn't like the buzz cut and would try to hide out from friends for at least a few days until my hair began to grow back.

Perhaps that's why, as a hippie in the '60s, I grew my hair long. At one point, my curly locks reached the center of my back. I had a lot of fun in my hippie days—perhaps too much fun. That undoubtedly contributed to me dropping out of college and ending up in the military in the late '60s. Fortunately, I did well on a code test, placing me as a communications expert in the US Navy Reserve. I spent a couple of years in Asia but did not have to engage in combat. Before going to Asia, I was assigned to a communications school. Attending the school required a high-security clearance, and the dress code was strict. Shoes and belt buckles had to be shined perfectly, and the length of hair, mustaches, and beards was strictly regulated. Hair, in particular, had to be cut short and was not allowed to touch ears or collar.

The hair regulation posed a problem for me: As soon as I graduated from communications school, I would go home on leave before heading over to Asia. I knew I'd see a lot of my hippie friends, and I did not want a regulation military haircut when I hung out with them. Hence, a couple of months before graduation from the school, I devised a plan to grow my hair as long as possible. There were routine inspections almost weekly, so I had to find a way to hide my increasingly long coiffure under my sailor hat.

Fortunately, I discovered a magic elixir: Dippity-Do hair-styling gel. I have no idea what was in that stuff, but it definitely kept your hair in place. All my classmates knew what I was up to. Most of them thought I was crazy to try such a daring scheme, but they thought it was hilarious and supported my efforts. More than once, someone warned me when a wayward hair was sticking out of my hat and, with their help, I managed to pass all of the weekly inspections.

Finally the big day came. I'd graduated from school with honors; all I had to do was pass the final inspection, and I'd be on my way home with an impressive head of hair. It was quite nerve-racking. My hair had grown so long that, even with Dippity-Do, I could barely hide it under my hat. Worst of all, the final inspection was held by the captain of the base himself, and he was famous for being a real stickler when it came to dress code and regulations regarding personal appearance. I'd heard of sailors who had been written up just for cracking a smile, and good luck to anyone caught with a smudge on his uniform.

On the morning of the final inspection, I wasn't taking any chances. I'd had my dress whites professionally laundered and ironed. The uniform was spotlessly clean, and the creases were so sharp it practically stood up by itself. I could see my reflection in my shoes, and my shiny belt buckle would blind you if you looked at it in the sunshine. Before heading for the inspection grounds, I spent a little too much time putting extra Dippity-Do in my hair in an effort to make it perfect. The last thing I wanted was to get to the inspection grounds late, so rather than walking there, I hitched a ride with a friend who was driving. As we were about to take off in the car, I noticed a few wayward hairs, so I opened the tub of Dippity-Do and put it on the dashboard to make some last-minute adjustments. Unfortunately, my friend accelerated too quickly and the open tub of Dippity-Do slid off the dashboard and landed upside down right in my lap. I sat frozen in terror as I watched the pool of bubbly bright-pink goo spread into my dress whites.

It was too late to try to do anything about it. I was wearing my only set of dress whites, and there was no time to go back to the barracks to search for another uniform. By the time I got to the inspection grounds, the entire lower section of my dress whites was iridescent pink. As I made my way to my place in the formation, no one who saw me could keep a straight face. The captain could tell something was wrong. Everyone in line seemed agitated, and the captain was getting upset. I heard him shout "Wipe that grin off your face, sailor" more than once as he worked his way toward my place in the line.

When my turn came, he was so shocked when he saw me that at first all he could do was sputter, but he finally managed to shout, "Sailor, what is that on your uniform?"

I shouted back, "Dippity-Do, sir."

Pandemonium erupted. Everyone in the line doubled over in uncontrollable laughter. Even the officers standing behind the captain broke into guffaws. The inspection was canceled on the spot, and I was escorted for a visit to the master-at-arms—basically, the base sheriff.

My trip home was delayed by a few days, as I had to pass a private inspection in the captain's office before I was allowed to go on leave. With the brand-new uniform I had to buy, along with my newly shaved head, I passed with flying colors. Although my leave was cut short, I still enjoyed the visit with my hippie friends, but I don't recall that they were overly impressed with my haircut. The master-at-arms obviously doesn't adhere to the rule of pruning and haircuts!

The Zen of Pruning

For many years I was a professional pruner, and among my favorite trees to prune were pines. That's because I had the good fortune of receiving private lessons on pine pruning from the grand master Tommy Kubota. Tommy was the son of Fujitaro Kubota. Born in Japan, Fujitaro emigrated to the United States in 1907 and created a number of famous Japanese gardens in the Puget Sound area, including at the Bloedel Reserve, the Rainier Club, the Seattle University campus, and the Kubota Gardens in South Seattle. Tommy worked with his father and was renowned for his pruning and design skills.

Tommy taught me that light pruning can be undertaken any time of year, but the best time to tackle major pruning on pines is in spring. This is when the *candles*—prominent upright buds on the ends of the branches—have expanded, but before the new needles appear. I also learned that there are a number of different ways to prune pines, depending on the outcome you want to achieve.

If you cut the candles in half, it causes them to bud and produce branching, resulting in shorter, thicker growth perfect for cloud pruning, a method where upward growth is removed and sections of foliage are trimmed to resemble clouds floating on the branches. On the other hand, if you remove some candles while leaving others uncut, the ones you leave will grow longer without branching, which results in uneven growth and a more natural appearance.

Another method is to thin pines by pruning back to secondary branches within the canopy. It's important to prune back to whorls where the branches originate. Pine branches will die if you cut them back to needles or bare wood. Thinning by removing branches in the interior of the tree exposes the character of the branching, giving the tree a venerable wizened look.

Tommy taught me to start at the top and work my way down, making small cuts. Big cuts were to be made only after considerable contemplation.

The hardest lesson for me to learn was patience. Tommy always said that pruning is an ancient art and that it takes time and thought to bring out the natural character of the tree. It also takes many years to transform a tree that has not been regularly pruned. It's unrealistic to expect a pine that you are pruning for the first time look as though you've been working on it for twenty-five years.

Despite the lessons from Tommy, I ended up learning the hard way when I pruned two very old mugho pines I discovered in an overgrown area in the back of the Seattle University campus. The pines hadn't been pruned for years. They were about 12 feet tall and so thick they looked like giant blobs. We were renovating the area where the pines were located, and I decided to sculpt them into spectacular centerpieces for the new garden.

Once I got started, however, I became so excited by how good I was making them look that I forgot all about taking my time to enjoy the Zen experience. The more I thinned out crowded branches and exposed the trunk and inner limbs, the more beautiful the form became.

By the time I was done, I knew I had overdone it. I had removed too many limbs. The sparse framework of twisted and gnarled branches that remained looked magnificent, but there was so little foliage, it reminded me of how I looked after my Navy boot-camp haircut. To my great consternation and shock, both trees died in about a year. Eventually I told Tommy what happened.

Instead of saying "I told you so," he simply smiled and said that, as in everything in life, experience is the best teacher.

Wisteria: Prune, Prune, Prune, and Prune Some More

I have a love-hate relationship with my wisteria. In May, when it's in full bloom and I'm sitting under the hanging 3-foot-long, magnificently fragrant flowers, I definitely love the tweetle out of it. Visitors go absolutely gaga when they see it flowering away in spring. It's growing on a trellis over our large square patio, and in spring there are always at least a thousand fragrant white-tinged-pink blossoms. Just as beautiful are the gnarled branches twisted around the pillars and side braces.

The hate part is due to the endless toil it takes to keep this behemoth under control. Don't even *think* about planting a wisteria unless you enjoy working your hinder off. If you are crazy enough to plant one, don't put it close to a house, garage, tree, or anywhere else its long-reaching tendrils can raise havoc.

Wisteria is one of the most aggressive vines you can plant in your landscape. Many years ago, my wife and I were in the market for a new house. We heard about a three-story house with a lake view for an exceptionally low price. We hurried over to check it out. Upon seeing the house, there was no doubt why the asking price was so low. There were two hundred-year-old wisterias, one planted on each side of the house. The huge vines had picked the three-story house up and pulled it off its foundation!

If the vines' aggressive tendencies aren't bad enough, wisterias can take forever to bloom. Many frustrated callers to my radio show complain that their wisteria has yet to bloom, even after twenty years. I can't figure out where they get their patience!

A number of problems can contribute to the lack of blooming. Wisterias need sun and don't bloom well if they're growing in shade. Also, pruning too hard late in the season can remove flower buds and deprive the plant of energy needed for flowering. The biggest reason that wisterias don't bloom, however, is incorrect pruning or total lack of pruning. Allowed to grow wild, a wisteria will put all of its energy into growth and forgo flowering for years.

Proper, timely pruning is the secret to getting wisterias to bloom. If your wisteria is in full sun and you follow the pruning system I'm about to describe here, your wisteria should bloom within four years. Just be aware, as I previously mentioned, you'd better like to prune, because if you use my method you'll be doing a lot of it for the rest of your life.

It all starts when you plant your wisteria. You'll need some kind of structure to grow it on, but make sure it's strong. The vines get big and heavy and, like a massive python, will twist around and crush any unsubstantial structure.

After planting, remove all but the three strongest vines. Wind those around and tie them to the stanchion you will be growing them on. Make sure you wrap the vines in the direction they naturally want to go. Japanese and Chinese wisterias naturally wind in different directions. The vines on Chinese wisteria wind in a counter-clockwise direction, while those on Japanese wisteria grow clockwise. If you try to force them to twine in the opposite direction, they'll rip the structure down and tie you to it in the process!

When the three vines wrapped around the upright stanchion reach the top, pinch the ends off to promote side growth. Once again, allow no more than three vines to grow along each cross brace, and wind and tie them in the same way.

To entice the plant into blooming, you need to do some special pruning. Wisterias normally bloom in mid-May, and soon after the blooming period is over, tendrils begin to grow out of the main structural vines that you've tied to the cross braces. For the first few years, your wisteria won't bloom because it's too young, but the tendrils will still begin to grow right after the normal blooming period is over. Each of those little tendrils is capable of growing 25 feet in one season.

The trick to encourage flowering is to cut back these rapidly growing tendrils to about 6 inches long. This is called *spur pruning*. All the energy that would have gone into 25 feet of growth is captured in the 6-inch spur and now stimulates flower bud production instead. Spur pruning is a lot of work that must be done every spring soon after the tendrils begin to grow, but pruning in this manner usually results in flowering within four to five years after planting.

While you're up there spur pruning, May is also the time to thin the branches. Once it's been there for a while, a healthy wisteria produces an incredible amount of foliage. As long as you prune it immediately after the spring blooms fade, you can remove about 70 percent of the twiggy growth without harming the vine or reducing bloom. Since my wisteria grows above my patio, I thin hard to allow air and light in.

Even if you're growing your wisteria along a horizontal trellis, however, thinning hard every spring will improve the appearance of the vine by keeping it from turning into a crowded rat's nest. While you're at it, this is also a good time to cut off the spent flower stems you'll find hanging down from the branches. That will prevent the big bean-like black seedpods from forming. The seedpods are poisonous—and in my opinion, unsightly. Removing the seedpods also encourages a second blooming in late summer.

As long as your wisteria is planted far from any structure or tree, often all that's needed to keep it blooming and looking attractive is a hard pruning in spring, followed by a light pruning after the leaves fall in November. If you were a dim-dim, on the other hand, and planted your wisteria near your house or valued trees like I did, you're in for a lot more work to keep it from causing big trouble.

The problem is that the vines don't stop growing. Within a month after the spring pruning is completed, new tendrils begin to grow again. I learned the hard way that these later-growing tendrils are just as vigorous as the first ones, and they're amazingly adapt at working their way under and ripping off house siding and roofing materials or getting entangled in nearby trees. My wisteria seems to know when I leave on vacation because whenever I'm away, it manages to slip its tendrils under the shingles of my neighbor's garage roof. I return home just before it rips the roof off. In order to preserve neighborly goodwill, I find that I have to prune my wisteria three to four times per year.

I follow up the spring pruning by climbing up to cut back the second wave of tendril growth in about mid-July. Then another climb up the ladder is usually needed when a third wave of tendrils tries to get into mischief in mid-August. The last pruning of the year happens in November, after the leaves fall. I go up one last time and spur prune the gazillions of wayward tendrils that grew after the late-summer trimming. Cutting back the tendrils in late fall will neaten the appearance and makes the bare vines look much more attractive in winter. Concentrate on mostly spur pruning and avoid overly thinning when performing the mid-August and late-fall pruning. Hard pruning at this time of year will greatly reduce blooming next spring.

Finally, once the late-fall pruning is completed, all growth will stop and you can sit back and appreciate the appearance of the gnarled branches, while looking forward to another spectacular flowering display next spring.

Don't get too relaxed. You had better eat plenty of brussels sprouts and work out regularly at the gym. You're going to need all of the energy and strength you can muster for the battle to keep the monster under control when growth begins again next spring!

The Fourth D of Pruning Should Be Decaf

A fair number of homeowners tell me that they don't prune their own fruit trees because they're worried that they'll do it wrong. Pruning fruit trees is hard work, but as long as you follow a few general rules, it's not all that difficult.

The key to successful pruning is timing and consistency. Fruit trees generally should be pruned both in summer and winter.

There's one exception. A fruit tree should be pruned when you plant it. The only pruning you do at this stage is formative. Don't make the common mistake of cutting back the ends of all of the branches to give the tree a round canopy. These *heading cuts* encourage major sprout growth. Head back too many branches, and you'll end up spending the rest of your life cutting off unsightly twigs that will grow out of the end of the branches right where you made the cuts.

The goal when pruning a newly planted fruit tree is to establish a sturdy, attractive branching structure and fix any minor problems that could cause trouble down the road. Remove any branches that are growing into the center of the tree. Also remove any branches that are crossing over and rubbing on larger limbs that could result in open wounds to the bark. Most importantly, check for *codominant leaders*. These are two similarly sized branches that grow vertically out of the same crotch in the tree. Choose the strongest one and remove the weaker branch, cutting it back to its point of attachment. Codominant branches develop weak attachment, and if allowed to remain, one or both of the branches are likely to break in a future wind- or ice storm.

The last and most important step when pruning a newly planted tree is to obey the law of haircuts and eating hot fudge sundaes: know when to stop!

Established fruit trees should be pruned two times per year. Summer pruning should occur from June until mid-August and should never exceed removal of more than one-tenth of the canopy. The object of summer pruning is to remove only shoots crowding the center of the tree. This will increase light into the canopy to enhance fruit ripening and will improve air circulation, thereby lessening disease problems.

Don't worry if the tree is full of fruit. If you take your time, you can still do summer pruning. As long as your TV cohost doesn't call to remind you that you promised to have a pear tree pruned to show on the morning news when she arrives in twenty minutes, you'll find that it's easy to remove all of the sprouts without knocking off fruit.

By the way, I got the tree pruned by the time she pulled up. Of course, there were only three pears remaining on the tree . . .

All other fruit-tree pruning should be done in winter, after the leaves fall and the tree is dormant. Even in winter, it's best to remove no more than a third of the wood, but if you are forced to remove a major branch, winter would definitely be the better time. Winter is also the best time to spur prune. This old gardening technique increases fruit production. Rather than removing sprouts completely, leave a 4-inch stub. The energy normally used for sprout growth is captured in the stub and initiates fruit bud production instead. In winter, you should also prune to maintain an upright branching pattern. Where limbs begin to bend downward, cut them to upright shoots.

Finally, in my opinion, the most important winter pruning job is to maintain the tree at a desired height by cutting back the tallest limbs to a node farther down on the branch. This is admittedly hard work, but don't make the mistake of letting this task slide for a couple of years in a row. Vigorous fruit trees tend to grow like wild banshees, and the branches at the top of the tree become thicker and harder to cut as they grow taller. Once the height of the tree gets away from you, the job of bringing the tree back down to a manageable size becomes much more difficult.

Controlling for height should not be confused with drastically lowering the height of the tree. Controlling for height usually entails cutting the tallest stems down by 6 to 12 inches, while drastically lowering a tree's height implies cutting the main branches down by a third of their entire height in one season.

Once the tree is the desired height, control for height every winter. That way, you will be able to make small cuts to control the tree height, thereby avoiding major cuts. Cutting large branches back by a third or more can shock a tree, throwing it into a downward cycle. Even if the health and vigor of the tree aren't too badly affected, your fruit tree will exact revenge by producing an unimaginable number of sprouts. These sprouts must be removed on a yearly basis or they'll block light, which will cause dieback in the lower branches and delay ripening of the fruit.

Another reason to avoid drastically lowering the height of the tree is because making large cuts will cause serious decay problems. There's always some decay where a cut has been made, but the bigger the cut, the more decay is likely to occur. Whenever possible, restrict the size of the cut to about the diameter of your arm. A fruit tree can easily wall off decay from small cuts, but large cuts usually end up with decay problems and may cause weakness down the road. No matter what size of cut, to help lessen decay, avoid cutting into the *branch collar*—the swollen section where the branch attaches to the trunk.

An important guideline to keep in mind when pruning fruit trees is to maintain a vase shape with upward-facing branches, rather than an umbrella shape with branches that hang downward. There is a hormone in all trees that stimulates growth at the highest point in any branch and impedes shoot growth farther down. On an umbrella-shaped tree, the growth hormone migrates to the top of the tree and causes what I call the Medusa effect: twelve gazillion water sprouts growing straight up, right out of the top of the tree.

These water sprouts are not only an unproductive waste of the tree's energy—because it would take years before they form fruiting spurs—they also block light needed for healthy branch growth and fruit ripening. Prevent the Medusa syndrome by cutting to upward-facing shoots or branches at the point where limbs begin to bend downward.

This technique can be used to renovate umbrella-shaped trees as well, but getting the ends of the branches to grow higher than the middle can take a long while. Sometimes, especially if an umbrella-shaped tree is old and in bad shape, it makes more sense to replace it with a new one. If you start with a tree grafted on dwarfing rootstock and prune it regularly, you should be able to easily maintain the tree to less than 12 feet tall. That beats the living tweetle out of having to climb a tall ladder to prune and harvest a taller tree that has gotten away from you.

There's one more important general rule when it comes to fruit-tree pruning. Actually, this rule pertains to pruning any kind of tree or shrub. The first task on any pruning job is to check for and remove what arborists call the Three Ds: dead, diseased, or damaged branches.

There are a number of reasons why removing the Three Ds is so important. First of all, you'll be surprised by how much simply removing the deadwood can improve a tree or shrub's appearance. Removing deadwood can also help prevent disease. Some diseases attack deadwood and then move into live tissue. Removing diseased wood by cutting back below cankers and swollen areas can prevent fungus or bacterial infections from spreading spores to healthy wood. Seriously injured or broken branches should always be cut back to a branch or major limb behind the damaged area, to prevent weak spots that might break in wind-, snow-, or ice storms.

Checking for and removing the Three Ds can save you a lot of embarrassment as well, as I found out back when I was a professional pruner. One of my favorite clients was an elderly woman named Ingrid. Every winter I pruned her huge apple tree, the pride of her back garden. It produced a good crop, but Ingrid loved its beautiful structure that she was able to admire while seated at her kitchen table.

Although I greatly enjoyed the artistic challenge of pruning Ingrid's tree, the real reason I couldn't wait to arrive at her house was because she always greeted me with a huge plate of the absolutely best homemade chocolate chip cookies on earth! Every year before I'd start pruning, we'd sit in her kitchen gazing out at the apple tree, catching up on gossip, while I'd devour several of her extra-large irresistible cookies and slurp down a couple of cups of her deliciously rich, strong coffee.

Unfortunately, one year I overdid it. I don't know how many cookies and cups of coffee I consumed, but I was so wired I probably could have forgone the ladder and simply levitated up into the tree's canopy.

I should have known I'd had too much coffee when we went out to the deck and I began jumping up and down while raving exuberantly about how spectacular the tree was going to look after

I finished pruning it. I literally ran to the tree with my ladder to get started. I began on one side and in no time I had both sides and the back done. I saved the front of the tree for last, and I knew just how I wanted to prune it to make the tree look fantastic when viewed from her kitchen window.

I climbed up to make the first cut and *snap*, the branch broke right off when I touched it. The same thing happened on the next one. To my horror, I realized that the entire major branch facing her kitchen window was dead and that I had no alternative but to remove it.

By the time I was finished, there was a huge empty gap right in the front of the tree. Had I checked for the Three Ds before I started pruning, I'd have noticed the branch was dead and I would have preserved side branches that would have covered much of the open space. The tree would have looked much better, and within a year or two, you barely would have noticed a major branch had died and been removed.

The happy ending to this story is that Ingrid didn't fire me on the spot and invited me back to prune her tree again the following winter. She even sent me home with a big bag of cookies. I'm happy to report that, after a couple of years of careful pruning, I was able to restore the tree to its former grace and beauty. From that day on, I've always checked for the Three Ds before I start any pruning job. As painful as it sometimes is, I wait to enjoy the coffee and cookies until after the work is done!

Take On the Tangled Mess of Forsythia

If you're not familiar with forsythia, it's the ubiquitous shrub you see everywhere in March, cheering the late-winter landscape with golden-yellow blooms. Despite its beautiful flower display, older varieties can be thugs. They often grow bigger than desired, taking over much of the garden. Without proper pruning, they can become a crowded, unsightly mess.

Homeowners and gardeners often try to get an oversize forsythia under control by shearing the top of the plant into a giant ball that resembles a Buhner buzz cut. The problem with this method of pruning is that where you cut, you get growth. For every branch that is cut back, two replacements will grow right out of the top of the ball to take its place. If you shear the top again the following spring, you'll get four new ones for every two you cut. At that exponential rate, if you keep pruning the same way every year, it won't take long for the number of sprouts to reach infinity.

The other problem with shearing only the top of forsythia is that every spring, new basal suckers grow into the canopy from the ground. If you don't do some thinning, it won't take long before the shrub becomes an unworkable tangled mass of branches.

To understand how to prune forsythia correctly, it's necessary to know how the shrub grows and where flowering occurs. Forsythia blooms on shoots and branches that grew during the previous season. Every year, after spring blooms fade, new shoots grow straight up without branching. The following spring, those shoots produce blossoms all the way up the stem, starting from near the base almost to the top. After the flowers fade, those shoots that bloomed in spring will branch out. Next spring only those newly grown branches will flower while the original shoot will never again produce blooms along the stem. Every year, smaller twigs will grow out of the previous year's branches, but only the new growth will produce blossoms in the following spring. Therefore, as seasons progress, older shoots become less productive and blooming occurs on ever-smaller twigs.

Since new shoots produce the best flower display, the most effective way to prune forsythia is to thin out some of the older unproductive shoots in order to encourage new ones to take their place. Every spring, immediately after the blooms fade, symmetrically remove about a third of the oldest branches by cutting them as close to the ground as possible. Thinning in this way will give the shrub an open, more attractive appearance, while increasing flowering.

If too many new shoots appear, thin them as necessary to prevent crowding. Resist the urge to lower the height of the plant by cutting back the top. That will only encourage sprouts to grow at the top of the branches and will ruin the appearance of the shrub. Left to grow naturally, the ends of the branches tip downward, giving the shrub an attractive fountain shape.

If you've neglected your forsythia or have been shaping it into a ball for years, it probably has become such a crowded mess it may be almost impossible to get your loppers in to make the thinning cuts. Once it's become unmanageable, the best way to deal with an overgrown, crowded forsythia is to cut the whole shebang to the ground and let it start over. It sounds drastic and scary, but having done it several times, I guarantee it won't kill your forsythia, even if you want it to.

The first time I used this technique to renovate a forsythia was right after I was hired by Seattle University. I had been on the job for only a couple of days when I was shocked to discover the biggest (and perhaps ugliest) forsythia I'd ever seen, right in the heart of the campus. The giant ball-shaped shrub was about 20 feet wide and 18 feet tall. The base was packed with tangled stems, and from the look of it, the canopy had been sheared so many times over the years, producing so many shoots at the top, that you probably could have walked on it. The thought of what it would take to get that monstrosity under control was terrifying, so I decided to put off dealing with it for as long as possible.

About a week later, while out working on campus, I noticed a group of agitated students next to the aforementioned forsythia. I headed that way, but an old priest who was walking by got there first. When he asked the students what was going on, they shouted, "Father, we think this person is dead!" That's when I noticed a pair of legs sticking out from underneath the forsythia bush.

The old priest told the students to stand back. Then, in anything but a gentle priestly way, he commenced to kick the tweetle out of the legs to see if there was any reaction. He shouted, "He is dead; call the rescue squad!"

I stood watching, in a mix of amazement and horror, as the rescue squad, siren blaring, screeched to a halt in the center of the campus. When the medics pulled the man out of the bush, he said, in a slurred voice, "What's everybody looking at?"

Evidently this man had been *living* under the forsythia in this heavily trafficked area of the campus for most of the summer. Not only did he have a bed under there, but also a table and chairs, and judging from the number of wine bottles, he had a lot of fun parties as well!

Needless to say, the administration was not pleased to learn that someone had made the forsythia in this key area of the campus his home. I knew that, before the week was over, I was going to have to cut the poor man's house down.

The only way to deal with a tangled mess like that giant forsythia was to cut all of the shoots right down to about an inch from the ground. I did it with a chain saw, which is extremely dangerous. It's safer to do this job with loppers, but if you have to deal with an enormous, crowded shrub like this one was, a chain saw will save a lot of time. If you ever need to do this type of chain-saw work yourself, be sure to rent long safety chaps that cover your boots.

Of course, when you cut all of the stems of a forsythia to the ground, you're removing the leaves that manufacture the food needed to support its often substantial root system. The shrub will exact revenge by sending up an incredible number of shoots in an effort to replace its lost food source. There are people who worked on my student grounds crew that year who still won't talk to me because they spent the entire summer cutting off the gazillions of unwanted suckers that grew up from the base. To keep the plant from turning back into a monster, I allowed only twenty-five well-spaced shoots to grow as replacements and removed all the rest. Those sprouts bloomed beautifully the following spring.

Every year since, as soon as the flowers fade, a third of the oldest canes are removed and only an equal number of new shoots are allowed to remain to take their place. By limiting growth in this way, the size of the root system decreases from lack of energy, and before long the number of new shoots produced will also diminish, making it much easier to manage. If you visit the Seattle University campus, find the flagpole at the corner of East Spring Street and Tenth Avenue. You won't believe that the lovely fountain-shaped forsythia growing there was the ugly monster that once tried to take over this beautiful area of the campus.

I never was able to find out what happened to the man who was so rudely evicted from his home in the forsythia bush. Knowing the Jesuits, they probably gave him a good meal and found him some temporary housing.

Pray for Your Rhododendron

One problem with rhododendrons is that when we see them for sale in the nursery, they're cute little shrubs with irresistible flowers. We bring them home and plant them where they'll really show off, often in front of a picture window. What we don't realize is that many rhodies are actually trees. I've seen rhododendrons over 50 feet tall in older European gardens. Before you know it, your cute little rhododendron grows large and blocks the view out the window.

Luckily, rhodies are among the easiest of all plants to prune. They have special hidden buds (*adventitious buds*), which are capable of producing branch growth anywhere you make cuts. The best time to prune is within a week or two after it finishes blooming. That's because it's important to get the pruning done early enough to keep from interfering with bud formation that occurs on new growth in mid-June.

Since you can cut them anywhere, one way to deal with a problem rhody is to cut it down to close to the ground. If your rhody is blocking the view or getting thin and leggy, and you're willing to go without flowers for four or five years, you can cut it down within a few inches of the ground and it will grow back thick and lush. Unfortunately, by the time it begins flowering again, it will inevitably have grown back to the same size and will once more block the view.

While you could move it, a big old heavy rhody is difficult to transplant. There is another solution, however, that will allow you to keep your rhody in front of the window so it won't block the view.

While working at Seattle University, I received a call asking me to help solve a dispute regarding this exact problem. Seattle U is a private Jesuit university, and the priests' living quarters surround a lovely private garden. The priests maintained their garden and only asked for assistance from my grounds staff if there was an unusual problem. There were two priests who did most of the gardening, Father Francis Bisciglia (Father B.) and Father Frank Wood, and they were almost always at odds about how things should be done. When they called me, I agreed to head on over, but I knew I'd be caught in the middle of what I'll politely call a lively discussion.

The problem revolved around a beautiful rhododendron that was planted square in front of the priests' chow-hall window that looked out onto the garden. The rhody was in full bloom, covered with spectacularly beautiful red flowers, but it had grown too tall and was blocking the view.

Evidently it was the first time it had bloomed in quite a while. That's because every five years or so, Father Wood would solve the view problem by cutting it down to 2 feet tall. By the time it grew tall enough to bloom again, it would once more block the view, so as soon as it was done flowering, Father Wood would once again put his pruning skills to work by cutting it back down to about 2 feet tall. In exasperation, the other priests suggested that the rhody be moved to where it could grow unimpeded so they could enjoy its blooms every spring.

Upon inspecting the rhody in question, I noticed that it had exceptionally attractive bark. That's not all that surprising: rhododendrons are close relatives of madronas and, just like their taller cousins, many have colorful exfoliating bark. The bark on the rhody in question was a peeling dark-red mahogany that was almost as showy as the flowers. Noting that the colorful trunks could be a year-round attraction, I recommended a different strategy.

Rather than moving it or cutting it back, I offered to remove the lower branches and twigs that were blocking the view, while allowing the canopy to grow tall where it would bloom up above the window. I'd begin by thinning the lower branches, offering a limited view through the leaves, but within a couple of years the top growth would be high enough to allow me to remove all of the lower growth. Before long, the garden could be viewed through a beautiful framework of colorful trunks, while the magnificent blossoms would bloom away in the canopy up above.

All the priests loved the idea, and everyone wanted me to do it, except one. Father Wood stated that for the last twenty-five years, it was his job to cut the rhody down every time it grew too large and he was going to do it again first thing next week. End of argument! Once Father Wood made up his mind, there was no changing it, so I headed back to my office disappointed.

The following Monday, to my surprise and bewilderment, I received a call from Father Bisciglia. He told me that Father Wood had been unexpectedly sent on a five-year sabbatical to Rome. "Get over here and prune that rhody *now!*" he said.

The pruning went just as I had hoped. The first year I thinned the canopy, and a limited view opened up. Then, by the spring of the second year, the rhody had grown tall enough to allow me to remove most all of the foliage blocking the view from the window. I preserved the most attractive trunks and branches while removing any that looked hacked back or unsightly.

By spring of the third year, I had created a magnificent view through a framework of beautiful limbs, while at the same time a stunning display of ruby-red blossoms covered the canopy above. As a final touch, I planted spectacular flowering, shade-loving perennials under the rhody. The whole display was magnificent, if I do say so my humble self!

A couple of years later, unbeknownst to me, Father Wood returned from Rome. He wasn't home for even one weekend before he cut the entire plant back down to 2 feet from the ground! I don't know if priests can go to hell, but if they can. . . .

PART 2

Wildlife: Domestic and Uninvited

Every Campus Needs a Pooch

I grew up in Wisconsin, and my family always had a dog. That's why I was excited when an opportunity came about to adopt a lost dog. I lived in a house with a fenced yard and had been working at Seattle University for a couple of years. While at a dinner party, a friend asked if anyone knew someone who wanted a dog. She had been to a doctor earlier that day, and he told her that he had found a nine-month-old puppy. He had fostered her for a few weeks. Despite queries to animal control and posting "found dog" notices, he was unsuccessful in finding the owner and needed to find a home for her.

Having grown up with dogs, I was super excited to meet the pup. I gave the doctor a call and agreed to come over the next day. The minute I saw the pup, I knew she was the dog for me. She looked to be half hound and half golden Lab, and she was well on her way to becoming her full size of 90 pounds. She had a gentle, loving personality and was incredibly beautiful, with golden fur and large brown spots that made her look like a deer. To my dismay, the doctor said that another person had come to look at her thirty minutes before me and wanted the dog, so I drove home empty-handed.

The next day, the doctor called me at work and said the other party hadn't come for her, so if I wanted the dog I should come and get her right away. I hopped in my car and drove to his office.

He seemed quite upset and told me he didn't want to see her again. He asked me to take her out of his car and take her away immediately.

I did as he asked, but as I was putting her in my car, I heard an odd sound. When I turned around, I realized the doctor was crying. It was obvious that he loved the dog, so I asked him why he was giving her to me.

He told me his wife hated dogs and she had given him an ultimatum: either the dog was leaving that day, or she was leaving that night. I told him he was making a mistake, and I took the dog!

I called her Goldie, the name the doctor had given her. I settled her into my house, and she slept well the first night. I didn't want to leave her alone when I went to work the next day, so I decided to make Goldie a campus dog by bringing her to work with me at Seattle University. The only problem was that I didn't ask anyone for permission.

The first day I brought her to the campus, it was snowing like mad and I was shoveling the walkways behind the Administration Building. We were right outside Father Sullivan's office window. He was the president of the university and wasn't known to be all that fond of dogs. Evidently he saw my good-size puppy knocking down students who were playing with her in the snow.

My boss called me later that day. He had received a call from Father Sullivan, who complained about Goldie on campus. My boss asked if I thought it was a good idea to bring such an untrained big dog to the campus. He went on to talk about liabilities and all sorts of other problems, but he never outright told me I couldn't bring her. I'm sure he assumed I'd get the message.

I knew that once I trained Goldie, she would make a wonderful campus dog, so I secretly kept bringing her. I couldn't risk letting my boss know, so I'd hide her in the bushes whenever I was working in areas where the wrong person might see her.

Then one day there was a big event being held on campus and all the trustees were invited. My staff and I had been working hard to get the campus looking extra-good, and I was driving back to the grounds shop in a work truck. Goldie was sitting on the front seat between me and a student employee.

As I made a turn in the heart of campus, there stood Father Sullivan and all of the trustees lined up right along the road. I had no choice but to slowly drive right past them. I grabbed Goldie and pushed her down on the seat and told the student to hold her there. But the student didn't have a good grasp on her, so when I raised my arm to wave at the president and trustees, Goldie came popping up between us. Everyone looked surprised, especially Father Sullivan.

Interestingly, I didn't get into trouble. I suspect a lot of the trustees were dog lovers and probably told Father Sullivan how nice it was that the university allowed employees to bring dogs to work. Either way, I figured the cat (OK, dog) was out of the bag, and I stopped trying to hide her and just kept bringing her to the campus.

Goldie came to work with me for her entire eleven years. She even had an entry in the university staff phone book: "Goldie Morris, Wildlife Manager." She was so loved by the entire university community, we had to put a "do not feed" sign on her to prevent overindulgent students and faculty from spoiling her with goodies.

Best of all, during her years as the campus pooch, I suspect even Father Sullivan got to like her. I'm fairly sure I saw him sneak a Milk-Bone to her a couple of times when he thought no one was looking!

Dogs: The Lovable Garden Pests

I had concerns when my wife, Mary, started searching for a new puppy after our beloved Kokie died at the ripe old age of fifteen. I remembered all the damage Kokie had inflicted on our garden when we brought her home as a pup, and with several tours of our garden scheduled, not to mention my frequent use of the garden as a TV studio, I was hesitant to deal with the havoc a puppy would wreak. I made the mistake, however, of visiting the puppy rescue with Mary. After she took one look at Fred, we were on the way home with a spirited little black puppy with a curlicue tail.

Fred lived up to my worst expectations. Within seconds of his feet touching the earth, our pea patch was history, replaced by an impressive hole. Fred was born to dig. In mere days, this canine backhoe dug more craters in our lawn than exist on the moon.

Of course, fools never learn. Soon we came home with little Ruby, an Australian cattle-dog mix. She was the perfect complement to Fred. Instead of digging, she ripped out any plant she could get her teeth on. When she needed a rest, she plopped her butt down on a rare ornamental grass, flattening it like a pancake.

Believe it or not, you can have a beautiful garden with dogs, even puppies. The key is to make a few changes that will ensure a fun life for your pups while protecting your special garden at the same time.

Before you bring a puppy home, determine where little Fido will be allowed to romp and play, and which areas are off-limits. I made the mistake of bringing Fred and Ruby home before I figured out how to keep them out of the special areas of my garden that are filled with rare and pricey plants. As an emergency measure, I put up a temporary plastic fence. Fred was a good boy and respected the fence, but Ruby saw it as a challenge. She liked to run through it at full speed, leaving the perfect silhouette of a puppy, including the shape of her Ross Perot–like ears.

I must compliment Ruby on her good taste, however. She always found the rarest and most expensive plants to rip out and toss gleefully into the air.

There are a number of ways that experts recommend to keep your pups out of the garden. Some work better than others. Invisible fences work well if you have an adequate-sized yard, can afford the expense, and are willing to do the necessary training.

A much simpler idea, often recommended by dog experts, is to stick a pole in the center of the garden with fishing line radiating off in all directions, tied to low stakes pounded into the ground at the outer edges of the garden. The idea is that Fido won't see the fishing line, but when he feels it, he won't like it, and he'll back right out of the garden. I tried it in the vegetable garden and it worked: Fred felt the line, didn't like it, and got out of the garden as fast as he could run. Unfortunately, he got tangled up in the fishing line first and dragged the pole, the fishing line, and every plant, including my precious nearly ripe brussels sprouts, right out of the garden along with him.

After that disaster, we opted to construct a cedar fence to keep Fred and Ruby out of the vegetable patch and my collector's garden. The fence we designed is constructed of only horizontal rails. It allows for an unimpeded view of the plants, while adding an elegant touch to the garden. Although the fence is less than 3 feet tall, it was easy to train the dogs not to jump it.

Don't fence your dogs out of every garden area, by the way. Instead, give them a few planted areas where they can play hide-and-seek. Plants such as caryopteris, lavender, cistus, rudbeckia, nepeta, and ornamental grasses are ideal for pet-friendly plantings because they are flexible, yet strong enough to bounce back after being trampled by doggy paws. Besides having room to play, dogs appreciate *rump spots*—a place in the shade where they can dig a cubbyhole for an afternoon siesta. The problem is that some dogs siesta in a new spot every day. To deter this, put attractive sizable stones among the off-limits garden areas to make them uncomfortable places to lie down.

A fence alone may not guarantee a beautiful garden. Well-loved pups who are treated like members of the family and receive plenty of attention and exercise are easier to train. They also tend to be better behaved than bored dogs, who can be mischievous.

Your garden, and quite possibly your furniture, could pay the price. Consider taking Fido to doggie day care or hire a dog walker (or ask a friend) to visit once a day to give the pooch some exercise and attention.

Don't expect to have a perfect lawn if you have pups. It's a waste of time to repair trails where the dogs constantly walk back and forth, and it's equally futile to repair damage caused by play in wet or shady areas. Replace the grass in these sections with smooth paving stones. They are attractive and lessen muddy paw prints in the house, and dogs love lying on cool stones.

The biggest complaint when it comes to lawn problems are the brown spots caused by dog urine. Basically the lawn is getting overfertilized. There are products to spray on the lawn to solve the problem, but I suspect you'd have to use them on a daily basis to be effective. The problem is much worse with female pooches. If you have a male dog, you might be able to solve the problem simply by planting a sacrificial juniper in a bed bordering the lawn. If you have female dogs, good luck.

Some dogs are born diggers. If your dog is like my dog Fred and won't stop digging holes in the lawn, try startling him by dropping a soda-pop can filled with a few pennies next to him when he digs. This method sort of worked with Fred. He didn't dig anywhere we put one of the cans, but he kept digging new holes, and soon there were so many cans that the lawn resembled a recycling center.

Much as we all want to have a beautiful garden, the most important concern is to make sure our gardens are safe for our pups. A good many plants are poisonous, especially to puppies, who tend to chew everything in their path. Ask your vet for a list of toxic plants, and remove them from pet areas before you bring your puppy home. Ask for a list of toxic houseplants while you're at it, as many of them are harmful to dogs if they chew them. Mushrooms can be a problem as well. There's no product that kills mushrooms, so during mushroom season in spring and fall, pull them out of areas where pooches have access. Be cautious with prickly plants as well. Remove any plants with prickers, such as rose, barberry, and pyracantha, or sharply pointed plants such as yucca that could cause serious eye injury.

Finally, don't use toxic pesticides where pups hang out. It doesn't mean you have to allow pests to decimate your garden. Use pesticides if you need to, but choose ones that are the safest for your pets. The newer iron phosphate–based slug baits such as Sluggo, Worry Free, and Escar-Go! have become popular because they are significantly safer to use around pets than are the ones that contain metaldehyde, but even these newer products can be harmful to dogs, especially if they eat a fair amount of them. Read and follow the directions on the label, especially regarding the amount to apply, and never create piles of it. Be careful where you store the bait. There are reports of pets opening cabinets, knocking packets off high shelves, even digging up piles of pellets that were buried. If you can't keep the pooches out of an area where slug and snail controls are needed, maybe it's better to go back to using some of the traditional pest-control methods everyone used before slug baits were available, such as "el kabotski." That's the method of pest control where you insert the slug or snail between your thumb and forefinger. Just remember to shout "el kabotski" as you squish.

I avoid chemical weed-control products in case of possible health effects. I prefer to pull lawn weeds or apply vinegar. You can try one of the dandelion digging tools offered on the market, but the ones I've used leave unsightly holes that can lead to a bumpy lawn, and worse yet, they usually cut the root, resulting in two for the price of one when the weed inevitably grows back. My favorite method is to blast them with straight white vinegar from the grocery store, but this method works only on a hot sunny day.

Of course, what it all comes down to is that dogs want to have fun, and no matter how well you plan, pups get into mischief. When that happens, just look into those loving brown eyes and you'll forget all about that irreplaceable $500 Wollemi pine he or she just trashed. Hey, it's only a plant.

If You Can't Beat Them, Eat Them

Squirrels are like brussels sprouts: you either love them or hate them. I'll be the first to admit that I'm not crazy about the ones that inhabit my garden. The gray squirrel common to the Pacific Northwest is not native to our region. According to legend, some fool trapped eastern gray squirrels in Central Park, New York, and brought them to Seattle for the 1909 Alaska-Yukon-Pacific Exposition. They escaped and, like the New York gangsters they were, took over the turf and kicked our native squirrels out.

Eastern gray squirrels can reach about 22 inches in length, including their long fluffy tail. I'm embarrassed to admit that I ate those things when I was a kid growing up in Wisconsin. My brothers hunted them (legally), and my mom had a rule that we had to eat whatever my brothers shot. Let me put it this way: they don't taste like chicken!

My problem with eastern gray squirrels is that they dig holes around every new plant in the garden and occasionally dig up newly planted treasures. They also raise havoc in ornamental containers. They're infamous for feasting on tulips and other spring bulbs as well. The birch tree growing in my neighbor's backyard has at least three squirrel nests in the canopy, and I suspect there might be multiple families living up there.

In case you're wondering, it's legal to kill gray squirrels, but it must be done in a humane manner. You are subject to fines if you cause unnecessary suffering to the animal. I have friends who trap and drown them. I don't know how humane that is, but there's no way on earth I could drown a squirrel or harm one in any manner. In Washington State, it's illegal to catch them in live traps and free them in a new locale.

Having said that, I admit I broke the catch-and-release law once. It happened in the 1980s when I worked at Seattle University. At that time, I was a regular on the *Northwest Home and Garden* TV show. My good friend George Pinyuh, Washington State University County Extension Agent, was also on the show. He had caught a squirrel in a live trap at his home, and somehow he talked me into showing us releasing it on one of our TV shows. We performed the illegal act on the Seattle University campus on TV for all the world to see. Not only is it a miracle that we didn't get fined, but the squirrel we released turned out to be quite the Don Juan. It had to be the most virile squirrel in the state of Washington. Within a year, the squirrel population at Seattle U tripled!

Since I have no intention of harming the squirrels that frequent my garden, I've learned to outsmart them in order to protect my plants. That's not as easy as it seems. In my ongoing battle with the varmints, I've had a few surprises along the way. For instance, I've always known that squirrels consider tulips a gourmet treat, but I didn't realize that they are just as crazy about crocuses. I found that out when I planted 250 of them on one side of the road at Seattle University. To my amazement, the next spring, almost all of them came up on the other side of the road. That experience taught me that squirrels are not only pests, but that they're kind of dumb as well. I'm fairly sure the reason the crocuses came up at all is because the squirrels forgot where they buried their snacks!

There are a number of techniques you can try to prevent squirrels from eating your spring bulbs. One of the easiest ways is to plant spring bulbs that are not appealing to those fuzzy little troublemakers. Snowdrops (*Galanthus*) are among the first to bloom, often coming up through the snow in early winter. Prized by collectors, these small but showy members of the amaryllis family are practically indestructible and form impressive-sized clumps over time.

Daffodil and narcissus bulbs are poisonous and therefore left untouched. Hyacinth bulbs also contain toxins that keep the squirrels away. A real charmer that squirrels leave alone is chionodoxa (glory-of-the-snow). It's easy to grow and, although the attractive blue flowers are small, they often reseed to form large colonies over time. Finally, a longtime favorite of mine is fritillaria. Squirrels never bother these unique and colorful spring bloomers. In fact, old-time gardeners often plant the bulbs of *Fritillaria imperialis* (corona imperial) in with their tulips, because the beautiful big orange and yellow flowers smell like a fox, thereby repelling squirrels as well as rabbits and deer.

That doesn't mean that you have to give up planting tulip and crocus bulbs. If your drainage is good, try planting your tulips 12 inches deep. Squirrels rarely dig far under the surface, so they aren't likely to reach the bulbs. Furthermore, tulips planted deeply often survive winter weather better than those planted near the surface. I've had colonies of tulips come back and bloom for more than ten years in a row. Planting deep, however, only works if you have well-drained soil. The tulips will rot if you try this in clay or hardpan. This method doesn't work with crocuses either. The stems aren't tall enough to make it to the surface.

Another technique worth trying is to surround your bulbs in a chicken-wire cage. The stems can easily find their way through the gaps in the wire, but the squirrels can't get to the bulbs. Unfortunately, when I tried this method, the squirrels exacted revenge by eating the flower buds right off the top of the stems as soon as they emerged from the soil. If you notice that happening, spray the buds daily with a hot-pepper spray. Simply add enough water to a supermarket ghost-pepper sauce to make it possible to spray from a spritzer bottle. Be sure to protect your eyes because that stuff is hot! All mammals except humans hate hot peppers. It's fun to watch the squirrels shout "*a-hoo-a*" before running away with their ears pinned back after taking a bite. Regrettably, that won't work in wet weather because the rain washes the pepper spray off the buds.

That leaves the final option: adopt a Jack Russell terrier or a wiener dog and make sure the first word he learns is "squirrel!"

I admit I've recommended dogs for pest control, but it's always tongue in cheek. That's why I was amazed when a viewer of my *Gardening with Ciscoe Live* TV show called back a few weeks after I kiddingly told her she needed to adopt a Jack Russell terrier to prevent squirrels as well as deer from eating her plants. Evidently she had taken my advice seriously and purchased a Jack Russell. She said she loved the dog, and he was doing a great job of keeping the troublemakers away, but nevertheless she was a little upset with me.

The caller lived in Alaska, where Jack Russells are scarce, so she paid an exorbitant price to have the dog shipped up from another state. Worse yet, in Alaska it's illegal to allow your dog to chase a deer beyond your property line. She said in the four months that she owned the dog, she had already paid six times more in fines to the county sheriff than she had paid for the pup in the first place!

In all truth, relying on a pet to control pests rarely works. When I was a kid, I would tie my big black Labrador, Thor, to my peach tree to stop the squirrels from stealing the fruit. The squirrels figured that one out in seconds flat. One squirrel would stand just beyond the dog's reach and taunt him, while another would sneak into the tree from the other side and knock the peaches down to their buddies, who would run off with them while my pooch was still preoccupied. Maybe squirrels aren't that dumb after all.

If you do take me seriously about adopting a dog to keep the unwanted wildlife away, I'm a big advocate for spaying and neutering pets. In my adult life, I've adopted five dogs that needed homes, and it saddens me that there are too many unwanted pooches out there. Still, I have to admit that when I was a kid, my family didn't always raise our dogs all that responsibly. I grew up in Wauwatosa, a fairly classy suburb of Milwaukee, yet back in those days very few of our neighbors ever spayed or neutered their dogs, and my family was no exception. We never neutered our big energetic Thor, but we justified it because we were careful to keep him from wandering the neighborhood, especially at night.

My dad didn't believe in allowing dogs to sleep in the house, so Thor slept in a pen in our backyard. Then one day a friend called and suggested we read the puppy section in the newspaper want ads. About halfway down the page we saw an ad for puppies at an address just down the street from our house. The ad read "Free puppies to responsible owners. Mother: gentle, loving Cocker Spaniel, Ginger. Father: dashing, fence-jumping Black Labrador Thor."

At first we thought it was just a joke, but just in case, that evening my mom and I hid out where we could see what Thor was up to in the pen. To our surprise, we watched that old rascal climb right over the almost 6-foot-high wire fence to escape. I suspect he was out all night quite often, but he was so smart that he would climb back into the pen just in time for breakfast.

After that, Thor was allowed to sleep in my bedroom. The bad news for Thor is that sleeping in the house put quite the damper on his love life. He had a great life though. He never did get fixed and lived to a ripe old age. I still have wonderful memories of that beloved pooch, even if he never could keep those darned squirrels from stealing my peaches!

Keep Bambi Out of the Garden

If you've ever dealt with deer in your garden, you know they're the equivalent of a 200-pound slug. They're one of the most destructive pests imaginable, capable of wiping out practically every plant in a garden in one night. People swear by folk remedies such as blood meal, Irish Spring soap, and even antistatic strips for the dryer, and of course there are a lot of manufactured products you can try as well. I found out the hard way, however, that repellents don't always live up to expectations.

Several years ago, a woman called my radio show asking how to keep deer out of her garden. At her wit's end, the caller explained that she lived right on a deer run and they were really doing a number on her plants. She barely had a garden left. I advised her that the only guaranteed way to keep deer out of your garden is to put up a fence or adopt a wiener dog. Deer will never jump over a solid fence they can't see through or over. For all they know, a Doberman could be waiting on the other side.

Even if deer can see through the fence, it will still stop them, but only if it's at least 6 feet tall. A fence at the bottom of a slope needs to be taller. Although they can't jump far, deer can jump high. I told the caller that if she didn't want to build a big expensive fence, deer fencing is another option. Deer fencing looks like bird netting but is thicker and stronger. It doesn't cost much, and if you use narrow fence posts, it practically disappears in the landscape, viewed from as far as 20 feet away. Deer can bust through it but rarely do, unless they're basically starving.

The caller didn't like the fence idea and wanted to know about using repellents. Although some repellents purportedly work fairly well, if you fail to reapply the repellent in a timely manner and it wears off, you can lose practically everything in your garden overnight. Another problem is that some deer seem to have poor olfactory nerves, or just don't mind the smell or taste of the repellent, and will feast on your plants even if the repellent is fresh.

After the caller hung up, obviously frustrated by my answer, the next caller stated that I didn't answer the question correctly. She informed me that I should have told the first caller to use coyote pee! When I asked her how they get the pee out of the coyote, she said she didn't know, but coyotes are natural enemies of deer and it really works. In fact, she was so sure I'd like it, she was sending me a bottle so I could test it and see for myself.

She followed through on her promise, but unfortunately the top of the bottle was not quite secure. The stuff sloshed all over the box it came in, and I'll never forget the look on the mail carrier's face as she handed me the box while telling me that if I was trying a new cologne, it wasn't a great choice.

Having no deer problem at my home or at Seattle University, I put out the word to my master gardener friends that I needed a test site. A woman named Mabel agreed to allow me to test the coyote pee in her garden. She was dubious of the chosen repellent, but she loved gardening and lived on a deer run where fences were not allowed, so she figured she had nothing to lose.

The coyote repellent came with little golf tees that had golf ball–size sponges glued on top. You dipped the sponges in the pee and then put them all around the perimeter of the property. The idea is that the deer would think that coyotes, their natural enemies, were marking their territory and they would avoid the garden. I ask you, what could possibly go wrong with a simple test like this?

Two days later, I picked up the ringing phone in my office to hear Mabel telling me to get out there and get those coyote things out of her garden, *now*! I hopped into my car, but the entire time I was driving out there, I couldn't figure out why she was so upset.

Once I got there, however, it took me about two minutes to figure it out. I still don't know how they get the pee out of the coyote, but I now know that it comes from coyotes in heat!

Evidently this product is a favorite of bounty hunters who use it to attract male coyotes. In this case it didn't attract any coyotes, but it worked really well with dogs. There were about eight male dogs in Mabel's garden. I tried to make them leave by shouting and chasing them, but they knew there was a female there and they weren't going anywhere until they found her. Worse yet, they sang love songs all night long: "*Eeeeeyowww!*"

Mabel hadn't been getting a whole lot of sleep, and she wasn't in a good mood. I gathered up all my little coyote sticks and got the heck out of there!

After about a week, I figured Mabel would have calmed down, so I gave her a call to find out if the coyote sticks worked. When I asked how she was, she told me to listen. I knew I was in trouble when I heard a very loud "*eeeeyowww*" coming from her backyard!

After I apologized profusely, I asked her if, while they were out there, the coyote sticks had kept the deer from entering her garden. Mabel replied with an emphatic "no." She said the deer had come right into the garden past the tees and eaten practically all of her roses and perennials in one night! I stated that it couldn't possibly be true as there were at least eight good-size male dogs hanging out in her garden.

"Those dogs couldn't have cared less," she said. "They were in love!"

There is one little epilogue to the story. Years later, a woman approached me after one of my garden talks. Although she wasn't a nun, this woman worked at a convent near Tacoma, Washington. The convent was in deer country and it had a beautiful garden. While at work one day, she noticed that the nuns regularly put out cups of pee to keep the deer away. Not long after she noticed this, the woman happened to attend one of my talks and heard me tell the deer and coyote pee story.

After hearing my story, the woman realized that putting out the cups was a waste of time and money. She wanted to warn the nuns, so she asked for a meeting with the mother superior.

"Ciscoe says coyote pee doesn't work to keep deer away," she told her.

"Well, nun pee does," the mother superior replied.

Oh, la la!

Scarecrows Are Scary

If you suffer deer, raccoons, or other nuisance critters, I have the tool for you to try. It's called a ScareCrow and generally costs around $70 each. The device consists of a head fastened on the top of a metal tube that you attach to your hose. The head contains batteries and a motion and heat detector. When an intruder is detected, the ScareCrow blasts it with a 35-foot stream of water, then reloads, preparing to fire again. The question is, Do they really repel deer?

The company that makes them sent me one to test, but I live in urban Seattle where there aren't any deer. I did test it on my pooch Kokie, however, and I can testify it worked great on her. I only had to pick it up and she would run for her life.

These products definitely do work if you use them correctly. A friend who lives right on a deer run in Olympia, Washington, explained that there are tricks to using them effectively. The first tip is to use more of them than the company recommends. In a mixed border filled with roses, perennials, and other deer delicacies, she uses four to protect a 2,500-square-foot garden.

In order to effectively repel deer, she discovered that it's necessary to relocate the ScareCrows occasionally throughout the day. That's because the motion and heat sensors have trouble detecting deer if they are facing the sun, so they need to be repositioned as the sun moves across the sky. The other reason to move them is, if they are left stationary for too long, the deer figure out how to circumvent the spray pattern. One thing's for sure: if you can afford using a few extras and are home enough to move them around, they really do the job. According to my friend, she hasn't suffered any deer damage for more than six years now.

People use ScareCrows to keep other unwanted animals from the garden as well. One common use is to keep raccoons from eating prized koi. Located strategically, and in adequate numbers, ScareCrows are very effective at keeping raccoons from getting to the fish.

Don't be in too big a hurry to pull the ScareCrows out of the garden, however. I talked to one young couple who had relied on them successfully all summer, but worried that the ScareCrows might break in the cold. When they heard a hard freeze was expected, they stashed them away in the garage. The raccoons must have seen them remove the ScareCrows, because there wasn't one koi left the following morning!

Another use for the ScareCrow is to keep heron from eating koi in ponds. That has proved less successful, however. I've heard that the herons send one bird to swoop down over the pond to make the ScareCrow fire, while another follows directly behind to skewer a fish! I'm sure that to be effective, more than one ScareCrow with careful placement is a must.

So although they are somewhat pricey, ScareCrows can be effective tools when it comes to preventing deer and other critters from harming the garden. I do have one last warning when it comes to using these tools. When you first set them up in your garden, don't forget they're out there. My TV cohost, Meeghan Black, and I showed how to use ScareCrows on a show we shot on Blake Island in Puget Sound. It ended up being one of the most hilarious shoots ever, because we kept forgetting they were out there in the garden. By the time we were done filming the show, we were both drenched. I can see why deer are terrified by these things!

Mole Control: Myths and Facts

Moles are perhaps the most hated critter in the garden. Although they aren't really that harmful to plants, they ruin the appearance of lawns by leaving their molehills everywhere. They can damage—and sometimes kill—small plants by tunneling beneath them and exposing their roots to air.

Contrary to public belief, moles don't eat plant roots. Voles (field mice) and other pests that do eat plant roots, however, may use the mole runs to gain access.

Moles are interesting creatures. They feed mainly on worms, insects, and other invertebrates. They've got quite an appetite: a typical mole weighs 5 ounces but can consume 50 pounds of worms and insects per year. Mole runs are really worm traps, because worms fall into the tunnels and moles find and eat them. They also save the worms for later. Their saliva contains a substance that can paralyze earthworms. The moles construct underground chambers where they store the paralyzed worms. That way, they always know there's a snack waiting for them after a hard day of digging tunnels.

Moles are quite the diggers. They can excavate tunnels at a rate of up to 18 feet per hour. They are speedy little creatures too, cruising through existing tunnels at 80 feet per minute.

Although it's widely believed that moles are blind, they actually have very tiny eyes, but since they spend most of their time in dark tunnels, sight isn't of much value to them. They also lack a good sense of smell or hearing, but they are so sensitive to touch and vibrations that simply striking the ground hard with a shovel close to a mole can kill it.

A friend told me that while she was out gardening, a mole popped out of the ground right next to her. Without even thinking, she grabbed it. When she realized what she had done, she screamed at the top of her lungs and threw the mole 20 feet up in the air. That definitely put the el kabotski on the mole.

Despite all of the mounds moles make, there are rarely more than five moles per acre. They're solitary animals and each mole has its own tunnel system. Except during mating season in late winter and early spring, there is never more than one mole per tunnel. The problem is that if you—or some critter such as a hawk or coyote—kill a mole, especially if you live in a rural area, there's always another one in the neighborhood that will move in to take its tunnel system. I've talked to farmers who tell me they trap more than forty moles per year!

Trying to control moles can become an obsession. In my early gardening career, I worked in a resort town on the North Cascades Highway in Washington State. The moles were constantly wreaking havoc in lawns by pushing up molehills and burrowing right under the surface. The town's head gardener was determined to put an end to the moles at any cost.

It was just like the movie Caddyshack. Under our supervisor's direction, we bombed them, gassed them, tried to drown them. You name it, we did it. The area looked like a war zone, but the only thing left untouched were the moles. I swear I could hear them laughing at our efforts.

According to research from several well-known universities, the only guaranteed way to control moles is to use traps. It should be noted here that using mole traps is illegal for homeowners in

Washington State, and if someone turns you in for using one, you could be fined. Having said that, most garden centers and hardware stores still sell them. If it is legal to trap in your area, check with experts on the best type of trap and how to use it properly.

Even if you live where it's legal, not everyone wants to go to all of the work of trapping moles. One of the best mole controls I ever had was my dog Kokie. She had terrier in her and would stay outside all night long, even in winter, hunting moles. If I heard a certain bark, I knew a mole was having a very bad evening. Unfortunately, the dog method won't work unless you have a fenced yard. I couldn't let Kokie out in front because there wasn't a fence, and she'd undoubtedly spend the night carousing the neighborhood with her canine buddies.

A cat, on the other hand, can be a different story. I had a neighbor who put her cat out only at night, luring him back inside every morning with gourmet cat food so he wouldn't hunt birds during the day. That cat caught every mole in the neighborhood for years. He finally died of old age about four years ago, and everyone in the neighborhood is still in mourning for him.

The problem is, How does one know if a cat will turn out to be a good mole hunter? About ten years ago, while working as a certified arborist, I visited a woman's house to determine if a big fir tree could be saved. During the consultation, I couldn't help but notice that there were an amazing number of molehills all over the lawn and garden. Then I heard a sound. It was her cat, Betty, struggling to make her way through the kitty door.

Betty was at least three times wider than she was long. To say that cat was well fed would be the understatement of the century. I told the woman that if she put Betty on a diet, the cat would catch the moles in her garden. When she replied dubiously, I expounded on my expertise on such matters and guaranteed it would work.

She took my advice and put poor Betty on a strict diet. That was more than ten years ago. Since that time, the woman and I have become friends and I occasionally stop by to see her. When I see Betty these days, I can hardly believe it's the same cat who could barely squeeze through the kitty door. She's slim and trim as can be.

To this day Betty has caught exactly zero moles. She's the laziest bum I've ever met. Not only that, but when I walk in the house to visit my friend, Betty growls at me. She knows I'm the guy responsible for her strict diet! I learned my lesson. Cats have the potential to be great hunters, but there is no guarantee.

There are quite a number of home remedies you can try using to repel moles. For the record, most of the folk remedies don't work. A good example is the often recommended idea of sticking Juicy Fruit gum down the mole hole. Evidently the mole is supposed to chew the gum, blow a giant bubble, and suffocate! What a crazy idea. Moles only eat living insects and worms; they don't chew gum.

A number of callers to my show told me they tried putting chopped garlic down the mole holes. At first it seemed to work, but in time the moles came back. Those evidently are the Italian moles.

Some folks tell me they've had success with either stuffing hair in the mole holes or spreading it all over the lawn. The hair evidently gets stuck between their toes and drives them crazy. I wanted to try it, but my wife wasn't too excited about letting me collect a bunch of strangers' hair from the barber to spread all over our yard. And what if it got stuck between our dog's toes?

Despite the fact that I meet folks who swear by them, those sonic devices that make sounds to drive the moles away don't work either. They seem to work at first, but the scientists at Washington State University tested every brand available and none were found to be effective in the long run. Some people swear that putting kitty bon-bons from the litter box down mole holes will keep the moles away. I think I'd rather tolerate the moles.

I've talked to several folks who have tried growing the mole plant (*Euphorbia lathyris*) in their garden to repel moles. The mole plant is a 5-foot-tall biennial that comes up one year and then dies the following year after it goes to seed. The milky juice is caustic and can cause nasty burns to the skin and eyes of humans and pets. Don't plant it. The mole plant reseeds like wild and will take over your garden. It only repels moles if you constantly cut the stems and put them down the mole holes.

Finally, for those of you who don't like my favorite veggie, spreading brussels sprouts on your lawn will not repel moles!

One method called Mint Mole Blaster has worked for me and for others as well, judging from e-mails I've received from folks who have tried it.

Make up Mint Mole Blaster as follows: Run a couple of big handfuls of pliable mint stems and leaves through the blender with just enough water to make a slurry. Then pour the blended concoction into a large soup pot about half-full of water, bring to a boil, and simmer for about thirty minutes. This will make a concentrate that can be diluted to make about 6 gallons of mole blaster. Whenever you detect mole activity, pour the diluted mixture into mole holes and around the surrounding area. The key to success is persistence. The moles evidently hate the smell of mint, and I've received a lot of e-mails from folks who tell me the varmints packed up their bags and moved to their neighbors' gardens.

As a side note: one caller swears that he used to have a major mole infestation and that sticking 8-inch-long crushed mint stems down the mole holes has totally solved the problem. He told me that his neighbors' gardens are full of moles but that his property has been mole-free for more than ten years.

Whatever you do, don't plant mint in your garden thinking it will repel moles. I don't know if it would work, but the mint will take over and become an even worse pest than the moles.

I should add here that some listeners have had luck using products containing castor oil. While some folks have had success with these products, others have not. I suspect the difference may be related to soil type or the depth of the mole tunnels. Either way, these products are expensive and the effects generally only last a couple of months before they have to be reapplied.

Local garden writer and good friend Ann Lovejoy swears by her mole recipe: two parts castor oil, one part dish soap. Mix together until foamy. Add 2 tablespoons of this mixture to 1 gallon of water. Spray in and around mole holes. I haven't tested this recipe, but it may be worth trying.

Finally, if nothing else works, you can learn to live with moles. There's no denying that they do a lot of damage to lawns when they first move in, but they aren't all bad. They aerate the soil and eat bugs. The trick to living with them is to never stomp the hills back into the mole run. If you do that, they'll just push back up to make another molehill. Instead, rake the soil out over the lawn or bed. Before long (in theory anyway) you'll rarely see any new molehills and hopefully you and the moles can coexist in peace.

Feed Birds, Not Rats

I'm wild about birds. We have a huge population of songbirds in our garden, and I've named practically every one of them, so it probably isn't surprising that soon after we moved into our current home, I decided to start feeding them. I experimented with feeding mixes but noticed that most of the birds preferred sunflower seeds and were tossing the millet, corn, and other seeds to the ground, causing a weed problem underneath. Hence I switched to feeding only with sunflower seeds. It was great fun watching the chickadees, nuthatches, and other resident birds take their turns at the feeder.

We often contribute tours of our garden to help raise funds for good causes. The money for the auctioned tour helps the nonprofit, and I have the fun of leading the winning bidders and their friends through the garden. If you're ever on one of my tours, expect to start the visit with a glass of wine in your hand. That way you'll like my stories even better.

On one of my tours, we had just sat down on the patio to talk gardening when I noticed a shocking sight. There was a huge rat crossing the patio arbor right above us! I quickly began to tell a really good story, hoping to distract attention, but I barely got started before someone saw it and pointed it out to the whole group. I'd never seen a rat in my garden before and practically died from embarrassment.

It just so happens that one of the guests that evening was an ex-mayor of Seattle. He told me there was no reason to be embarrassed. He said that when he was mayor, Seattle was the number-two worst city in the nation when it came to rats. I don't know if Seattle still rates that high, but there is little doubt that rats are abundant in the Seattle area.

Since it was the first rat I'd seen in our yard, I began to wonder what had attracted it. It didn't take long to find out. A couple of days after the arbor incident, I spotted a rat on the bird feeder. Not long afterward, we saw more congregating under the feeder to feast on leftovers that fell to the ground. My wife asked me to stop feeding the birds, but I wasn't ready to give in. I visited a local bird supply store and came home with what was supposed to be a rat-proof bird feeder. I was pleased with the compromise.

But when Mary came home the next day to find the hind end of a very well-fed rat sticking out of the portal of the rodent-proof feeder, I knew my days of feeding birds were over. I feared that if I removed the feeders, the birds would leave the garden, but fortunately our garden contains a wide variety of plants that provide food and shelter. The garden is also multilayered with trees, shrubs, and perennials growing to varied heights. This provides nesting sites preferred by different kinds of birds. I never spray pesticides that could be harmful to the birds or the insects they rely on as a food source. I am not quick to tidy up the garden in the fall, so as to leave seedpods for the birds. I also brought in a few extra birdbaths and fountains to make sure there was plenty of water for drinking and bathing. To my great relief, despite removing the feeders, just about all of my bird friends stayed put in the garden.

Before long, I found that watching the birds frolicking in the birdbaths was just as much fun as viewing them at the feeder. I did get one harsh lesson though. I had located my birdbaths in the open, away from places where neighborhood cats could sneak up on them, but I hadn't considered that birds of prey can also be a problem. One day I was watching Charlotte Chickadee frolicking in the bathwater when, out of nowhere, a sharp-shinned hawk swooped down and snatched her right out of the tub.

That sure taught me a lesson: place your birdbath away from shrubs where cats can hide, but give it a bit of overhead cover so that a hawk doesn't have a straight shot at it. I'll never forget hearing Charlotte's "*Eek*" as the hawk flew away with her! I'm happy to report that after moving the birdbaths under cover, I've never lost another of my little avian friends to a hungry hawk.

Don't Invite Unexpected Guests into Your Compost Pile

At our house in Seattle, I had an open compost pile. Basically it was constructed of three solid walls and open in the front. I must say I make pretty good compost, despite the fact that I'm not all that scientific about how I do it. I basically follow the one-third/ two-thirds rule. The goal is to add one-third green matter (manure, food scraps, leafy materials like lawn clippings and green leaves) to two-thirds brown materials (branches, stems, dried leaves, peels, bits of wood, fine bark sawdust, shredded brown paper bags, coffee filters, conifer needles, eggshells, hay, peat moss, wood ash).

I really don't worry about getting it perfect or putting it in layers. I just follow the recipe and mix it up all together, and it seems to work fine. It's important to keep the material in the bin about as moist as a squeezed sponge. Accomplish this by covering the material with an old rug. It helps hold moisture in during summer (you might have to wet it a bit from time to time in hot, dry weather) and in winter it keeps excess water out, preventing the compost from getting sopping wet.

I admit that I may have been a bit careless about what food scraps went into the bin over the years. Some stale bread and maybe a few pieces of cake may have found their way into the mix, but the key to success (and preventing unpleasant odors) with an open system like this one is to turn the pile often. As long as I turned it every two weeks or so, the pile cooked nicely and there never seemed to be any problems.

That is until one afternoon when I stuck the fork in to turn the pile. The rat that came charging out was huge and looked like a miniature pitbull! You'd think that my terrier mix Kokie, who was standing right next to me, would have given chase, or at least fought to save me from this beast. On the contrary, she led the way as we both ran screaming for our lives!

I'm often asked if it's OK to put items like old bread and veggie scraps in your compost pile. Usually veggie scraps are acceptable, but these days I make sure to leave the leftover bakery goods and anything tasty like that out, unless there's no way a critter can gain entry.

If you want to compost food scraps, you're better off using a closed system such as a tumbler bin, made of a drum equipped with aeration holes that can be turned regularly. Another option is a worm bin. Kids love worm composting. It's easy to make your own worm bin: Use practically any size wood or plastic container. Drill plenty of holes in the bottom, and make sure there's a tight-fitting lid to keep moisture in and pests out. Order red worms (available online) and give them a nice bed of moist shredded newspaper. Every three to six weeks, move the compost to one side and in the cleared space, put down some new bedding. Within a month all the worms will move into the new bedding and you'll be able to harvest the rich worm compost. Don't be intimidated about handling the worms. They are a lot less frightening than the critter I encountered in my compost pile!

Learn from Your Elders

Now and then I meet people who come up with ingenious solutions to garden problems. That was the case when I gave a talk for one of the garden clubs in the Seattle area. When I arrived, everyone in the club said I had to meet a special ninety-three-year-old woman renowned for her gardening skills and creative garden ideas. I was soon to learn that she was quite a character as well.

Not long after I began my talk, someone asked how to rid their garden of wasps that were nesting in the ground in the middle of her garden. I gave the standard "spray them with one of the aerosol pesticides at night" answer (see The Bald-Faced Truth, page 94), then noticed the ninety-three-year-old woman raising her hand.

She had her own method to deal with wasp nests: she attaches a long extension cord to an electronic mosquito zapper. Mosquito zappers are those lights that are supposed to attract mosquitoes and fry them when they hit the electronic core. Next she ties a long rope to the zapper and throws it over a branch on a tree near the nest. Then she swings the zapper to crash right on the hole where the ground nest is located. She said that when the wasps come out in force to do battle with what they think is an intruder, it sounds like a Rice Krispies symphony. Before long the zapper wipes out the colony.

I've never tried that method, but I have to admit it might work in the right circumstances. Not long after the wasp question, a different woman asked if I knew of a way to keep crows out of her garden. Crows had taken over her backyard. They were noisy, dive-bombing both her and her dog, terrorizing other birds, and even attacking nests and eating baby songbirds. After I admitted I had no idea how to make crows go away, the older woman's hand shot up again.

"There's an easy way to get crows to leave your garden," she said. "First, you go out with your shotgun and shoot one."

When I asked if that wasn't illegal, she said that she only shoots one and no one tells. When I asked who shoots it, she answered, "I'm a crack shot, sonny, don't give me any lip!"

She then said that she takes the dead crow and lays it in the middle of her garden, and all the crows from miles around come to have a funeral for their dead comrade. Then they suddenly all fly away and, according to her, they don't come back for about six months.

"So what do you do when they come back?" I asked somewhat testily. "Go out and shoot another one?"

"No, you dummy," she said. "You throw the crow in the freezer!"

I got a chance to test her advice while at Seattle University. One of the gardeners told me he had just witnessed a crow getting electrocuted. Evidently it landed on some bare wires and got zapped. It was still out in the garden, where it was lying with a very surprised look on its face. He was going to bury it, but I told him I needed it for an experiment.

I placed the unfortunate bird in a garden heavily frequented by crows. Sure enough, several crows flew in for the funeral. They stayed for about fifteen minutes and then all at once they flew away. The crows didn't return to that area of the garden for at least several weeks. And no, I did *not* throw the crow in the freezer!

PART 3

The Secret Life of Insects

The Epic Story of IPM at Seattle University

I began working at Seattle University on the first day of spring in 1978. I was hired as a foreperson. The grounds department was run by an old priest who we all called Father B. He was a wonderful person but didn't like managing, so he allowed me to take on the day-to-day running of the department. Prior to working at SU I had worked at a number of commercial landscape companies. In those days, you were expected to spray first and ask questions later, but I was never at ease with this mentality. When I began my job at SU, I was determined to garden in a more environmentally friendly manner.

That's why I was so surprised when, not long after I began working there, I walked out of my office to see someone spraying the campus trees. When I asked him who he was and why he was spraying my trees, he said he was Ed, the campus painter. Evidently he was also the self-appointed campus exterminator. He didn't know what bugs he was trying to kill, but it didn't really matter. His motto was "the only good bug is a dead bug."

Ed informed me that he sprayed most of the campus trees at least four or five times a year, just in case there were a few critters who survived the last go-round. It was evident that health and safety were not Ed's major concerns.

Ed was spraying diazinon (a pesticide later pulled off the market for health concerns) in the middle of a weekday when school was in session. Furthermore, he was using a makeshift trailer-mounted paint sprayer that siphoned the pesticides out of two open 50-gallon drums. Students were running for cover to get away from the spray, and every time the trailer bounced over a speed bump, diazinon sloshed into the street and down the storm drain.

By the way, Ed used the same sprayer to paint the buildings, so the walls were definitely bug-free.

I met with Father B. and we both agreed that we couldn't allow Ed the painter to continue as the campus sprayer. Unfortunately, there was no budget allocated to contract a spray service, so I had to take over the program. I had been a gardener for many years, but I had never used a power sprayer. The campus was famous for its spectacular collection of specimen trees, and I was terrified that an untreated pest might do some of them in. My first decision was to buy a professional-grade sprayer. I also insisted that all spraying had to be completed by six-thirty in the morning, well before the students arrived on campus.

In the spring of 1981, Father B. retired and I was appointed director of the grounds department. Around that same time, I attended a WSU County Extension seminar on integrated pest management (IPM), a new method of pest control. The goal of IPM is to move away from calendar sprays where pesticides are applied at the same time every year as a protective measure. With IPM, a gardener tags branches on a given number of plants and then monitors them on a regular basis to determine if harmful insects are building up to damaging levels. The gardener takes action only if the number of insects reaches a predetermined number. A major difference is that instead of reaching for the sprayer, if possible, the gardener uses alternative methods.

The first line of defense is to take proper care of the plants. When a plant is growing in proper soil and exposure, with a correct water and fertilizer regimen, it is more resistant to problems including insect pests. Choosing plants that are resistant to common pests or diseases can also prevent future problems. If at all possible, the gardener uses mechanical controls to keep insect pests under control. Methods include screening plants to prevent infestation, handpicking insect pests off, blasting them off with a powerful spray of water, or squishing them.

Another alternative is to bring in beneficial insects to eat or parasitize harmful ones. In the same vein, making life good for beneficial bug-eating insects and birds that reside in the area can make a big difference with insect control. Finally, if no effective alternative can be found, spraying is permitted, but the pesticide used must be the least harmful to humans, pets, other animals, and the environment.

Even though the seminar was geared to farmers, I realized that IPM was a common-sense approach to dealing with pests in an ornamental landscape. As I was driving back to SU from the seminar, I began to formulate an IPM plan. We'd have to monitor spruce trees, birches, and a few other trees and shrubs that were subject to serious infestations, but most plants on campus were generally not susceptible to pest problems.

When I arrived back at the campus, I called my gardening staff together and told them about IPM. As I expected, all of the gardeners were excited to give it a try. Hence I made my first big decision since being put in charge of the Seattle University grounds department. I put a stop to all spraying until I could devise an IPM plan.

I hadn't, however, thought about the problems this might cause. Ed's nonselective spray program had wiped out the good bugs along with the bad ones. Bad bugs return much more quickly than do beneficial insects. There's always plenty of food for harmful insects to feed on, and most don't even need to mate in order to reproduce in great numbers.

Beneficial insects, on the other hand, build up populations slowly. They have to fly to your area and find enough food to make it worth staying, and they reproduce slowly. My decision to stop spraying, coupled with the fact that there were so few beneficials left on campus to keep troublemakers in check, enabled aphids and other harmful insects to build up to incredible populations quite quickly. By the end of summer, aphid populations exploded. Their honeydew (polite word for liquid bug poop) rained down from the trees, giving anyone who walked under the tree a free Dippity-Do treatment.

My new pest strategy didn't go over terribly well with the administration, and I was summoned for a meeting with the vice president. Father Hayes was rightfully upset about "the major bug problem" on campus and said he had even noticed students walking into class with bugs in their hair. Needless to say, I didn't mention the aphids I noticed in his coiffure.

I told him that, with winter coming, the bugs would soon disappear for the year. We talked about the health and liability problems that could occur by allowing someone like Ed the painter to spray. Then I told him about the safer, more environmentally friendly pest control program I was planning to implement on campus.

Father Hayes was OK with the new program if it worked, but he wanted to know exactly what I was going to do to make sure bugs didn't take over the campus again next spring. Without thinking, I blurted out that I was going to bring in good bugs to eat the bad ones.

I still remember Father Hayes's words upon hearing my idea: "The campus is infested with bugs, and this maniac is planning to bring in more!"

We discussed my idea for at least a half hour, and somehow I talked him into it. He gave me permission but he added one condition: if my cockamamie idea failed and students were once again covered in aphids and sticky bug poop, he'd find someone else to run the department!

I left the meeting a nervous wreck. I had no idea if an insect release would really work. My original idea was to release ladybugs (also known as lady beetles). It's easy to buy ladybugs and they're renowned for eating aphids.

After researching the idea, however, I realized ladybugs wouldn't work. These insects go through a metabolic change in fall and fill their bodies with fatty oils that serve as antifreeze. As temperatures drop, ladybugs fly to the forests and mountains where they find a hole under a rock or log and send out pheromones to attract their brothers and sisters to join them. The ones who get there early are warm and cozy surrounded by the other beetles, while those who procrastinate freeze their little wings off at the edge of the ball.

The vendors who sell ladybugs to us know where they hibernate. They scoop them up, keeping them in cold conditions until selling them to us in the spring. When we release them, the beetles are still full of fatty oils and can't eat until they work them off. Since ladybugs don't do push-ups and sit-ups, they fly for exercise and land 2 to 10 miles away, where they will begin feeding to help control someone else's aphids. Although still beneficial to the neighborhood at large, they won't help control aphids in your own garden.

There was another problem that might cause the plan to fail as well. The trees were full of ants. They were up there because they feed on the honeydew from the aphids. Ants are tough guys in the insect world and fight to protect their food source. I actually saw ants kill some of the few ladybugs remaining on campus when they tried to feed on aphids.

I almost gave up on my idea to bring in good bugs; then I learned about an insect called a lacewing. The green or brown adults are approximately ½ inch long. They hold their lacy wings over their backs like a church roof when resting and can often be seen flying around porch lights in fall. In nature, the female lays her eggs at the end of strings that she produces for that purpose. Placing her eggs on top of the strings makes it difficult for predators to find them. More importantly, the voracious lacewing larvae would gobble each other up the minute they hatched if they could get at each other.

Lacewing larvae have an ingenious method to enable them to get past the ants' defenses. Right after hatching, the fast-moving tiny larvae run down the string. As soon as a larva spots an aphid, she sticks her hollow feeding jaws into the hapless victim, picks it up, and sucks the juice right out of it like a living milk shake. Instead of throwing the aphid body away, the lacewing larva throws it on her back. A sticky substance, probably bug poop, allows the aphids to stick. The larva nabs another aphid before the ants spot her, and then another. Within minutes of hatching, the lacewing larva may have three or four aphids on her back. Now she can sneak right by the ants. The ants seem to think, "Look at those stupid aphids sitting on top of each other." They don't even notice mademoiselle lacewing beneath in her clever disguise.

I knew that it was possible to buy lacewing eggs, but I couldn't find a supplier. It was before the internet had evolved to the point where you could purchase them online. Fortunately, I had joined an amateur entomology club, and a bug broker (there really is such a profession) came to our meeting. He told me he could supply me with the lacewing eggs, but he warned me that there often were delays and it might take a while. He told me to monitor the birch trees closely and to call him at the first sign of aphids. If the aphid populations grew too large before I did the release, it might be too late for the beneficials to gain control.

For some crazy reason, I took the leap and ordered more than 20,000 eggs to be delivered when needed.

The following spring, I kept a close eye on the birch and other susceptible campus trees. Through all of April into early May, I didn't see one aphid. I began to think maybe they weren't going to show up that spring. Then I left for a week of vacation, leaving my second in command with strict instructions to monitor closely and call the bug broker at the first sign of trouble.

I got back on a Monday and, when I walked out of my office door, honeydew hit me right in the face. My second in command insisted it hadn't been there the previous Friday, but either way, it was time to act.

I immediately gave the broker a call. He said he was having trouble getting the eggs and that it could take up to three weeks. By then it would be too late.

I began to consider spraying. Then the broker told me that he had an almost equally large stash of eggs that a public institution had ordered but were not allowed to release. When I asked him if something was wrong with the eggs, he said he'd been holding them too long and a good number of the eggs might have already hatched. I asked what all good managers would: "Will you give me a discount?" When he said yes, I asked him to bring them over to me pronto and they arrived in less than an hour.

I gathered my staff together. The eggs came in little round 5-inch-diameter boxes, each containing hundreds of eggs surrounded by rice. We all screamed in unison when we opened the first box. Gazillions of larvae had hatched and were eating each other in a wild frenzy. I shouted, "Grab the ladders and let's go!"

Releasing insects isn't as easy as it sounds. My job was to pour some of the rice containing the eggs (and hatched larvae) into our prepared containers. These were small paper cups with holes punched in the bottom to prevent rain from drowning the eggs. The gardeners climbed into the trees and stapled the cups onto the branches.

The prescribed method is to put the eggs out just as the first few larvae start to hatch, but in this case the majority of the eggs had already hatched and the larvae started biting the living tweetle out of us. It hurt like mad, but since the larvae were so small, the pain didn't last too long. I can't tell you how happy we were when the last of the lacewing eggs and larvae were released at the end of the second day.

At first I thought the experiment was a failure. At the end of the first week, the aphid population seemed to keep growing, and the amount of honeydew raining down seemed to be increasing. By the middle of the second week, however, I started spotting lacewings in their clever disguises and the amount of honeydew appeared to be decreasing. By the end of the third week, I knew we had won the battle. The aphid population crashed and the ants left the trees for lack of a food source. A few aphids remained, but that's exactly what I'd hoped for. My ultimate goal was to develop a balance of nature. To achieve this, some bad bugs must survive in order to feed the good bugs.

Buoyed by my success, for the rest of that summer, I carried those little plastic 35 mm film canisters with air holes poked in the top. If I found lady beetle larvae, I relocated them to the campus. Since lady beetle larvae can't fly until becoming adults, they remained on the campus trees to help with pest control. Although the adults migrated as expected in fall, judging from the huge populations we developed on campus over the next couple of years, I'm convinced they remember where they came from and return the following spring.

The lacewing release turned into one of the first highly successful campus IPM programs in the nation. With the help of my talented and dedicated staff, we developed all kinds of innovative methods to deal with pests, plant diseases, and even weeds. We were the first college campus gardening program in the Pacific Northwest to eliminate the use of all chemical pesticides, including herbicides. By making the campus a welcoming place for beneficial insects and birds, we were able to achieve the balance of nature we had hoped for, and the SU campus was the first in the state to be designated a wildlife refuge by the Washington State Department of Fish and Wildlife.

The environmentally friendly gardening program we developed not only helped Seattle University win several prestigious national awards, it has been written about in national publications and study aids. The insect release and our ongoing environmentally friendly gardening program have been highly popular with the entire community as well. Even though it looked for a while like I might lose my job, the release was so exciting, I'd do it all again.

Remember, if you try this at home, put out the eggs before too many of them hatch. Those little rascals really do hurt when they bite!

Don't Lose Your Head Over Crane Flies

Years ago, a friend from Forks, Washington, called me to ask my opinion about the grayish things all over his lawn. I assumed it was some type of seedpod falling from trees and, since I was going to visit my friend in a few days, told him I was sure it was nothing to worry about. I'd check it out when I arrived.

When I drove up to my friend's house, he was standing in front of a patch of mud that had been his lawn, giving me the "I thought you're supposed to be a gardening expert" look. In the four days since our phone conversation, his entire lawn had disappeared, leaving only a muddy mess where the turf had been. Upon inspection, we found close to a hundred crane-fly pupae per square foot!

Of course, if you had seen the lawn before this happened, you'd know that the crane flies did him a favor. The lawn was a horrible wet mess that needed replacement anyway, and now the job would be all that much easier.

European crane flies have become a pest in Alaska, British Columbia, Washington, and Oregon. They are also in Nova Scotia, Ontario, and New York and are gaining a foothold in many other states as well. The adults resemble giant mosquitoes. Their bodies are about an inch long, and they have fragile long legs. They are clumsy fliers and often brush against people when in the house. They entertain me because my wife never fails to scream when she feels one brush across her face in the middle of the night. In the right circumstances, they can cause severe damage to lawns, yet it's rarely necessary to spray chemical pesticides to keep them under control.

The larva that begins as a small white maggot eventually develops thick gray skin and can grow to as long as 1½ inches. The larvae feed on the roots of lawn grass. If they build up into high numbers, they can cause serious problems. I've seen what they're capable of.

Fortunately, massive crane-fly damage like this is by far the exception. Recent studies have found that it takes a lot of crane flies to seriously harm a lawn. If there are up to twenty-five larvae per square foot, the damage is usually minimal. Even if there are up to fifty larvae per square foot, if your lawn is in relatively good shape all that's needed is a bit of fertilizer, and the lawn will bounce right back.

Populations of over fifty larvae per square foot usually require some form of treatment to prevent noticeable damage, but the good news is, populations of that size are quite rare. The master gardeners in Whatcom County have been monitoring lawns in their area for a number of years. In 2001 they found that most damage attributed to crane flies was actually caused by other problems such as thatch buildup, compaction, fungus problems, or improper maintenance practices. Of forty-five lawns surveyed thought to have crane-fly damage, 65 percent had no crane-fly larvae, and only about 5 percent had over twenty larvae per square foot.

Interestingly, many of the same lawns that had crane-fly populations when they began monitoring in 2001 were found to be completely crane fly–free by 2004. No one is sure why. It could be that beneficial critters are controlling them for us. More recently, turf researchers in Washington and Oregon have said that only

10 percent of lawns will get a crane fly, and only 1 percent of lawns will need treatment.

Crane flies are attracted to, and cause the worst damage on, lawns that are constantly wet. If you've got soggy conditions and you've got crane flies, you're going to have them again next year. That's because female crane flies mate soon after they emerge from their pupa cases. Within a day or so, she forms about 350 eggs within her. In fact, she's so heavy she can fly only about 8 feet before laying a significant number of the eggs.

The adult crane flies emerge in large numbers in mid-August through mid-October. Don't freak out and grab the bug spray if you see lots of them flying or gathering on fences or the side of the house. They can't bite or harm you in any way, and they probably have already laid their eggs by the time you see them. One thing you can do is to stop watering your lawn to dry it out a bit. The eggs need a fair amount of moisture to survive.

Crane-fly damage occurs in March through mid-May when the larvae gain size. The damage doesn't usually become visible, however, until May or June, when the larvae have formed pupae and are immune to pesticide sprays. The best way to see if you have a problem is to look for irregular yellowing patches in the lawn starting in March. Find out how many larvae are present by pouring warm water on the soil surface where you suspect crane flies may be causing damage. The larvae will come writhing to the surface, allowing you to count their numbers. Note how many there are per square foot.

If, after monitoring your lawn in spring, you find there are damaging levels of the larvae, there are a few alternative treatments that are effective at reducing population levels. Beginning next fall, if you see lots of adults flying about or gathering on walls or fences, stop watering your lawn. Your grass will brown out a bit, but it will survive until the fall rains begin. Drying out the lawn can break the crane-fly cycle of coming back year after year, because as I mentioned earlier the eggs must have moisture to survive. Eggs laid on dry soil usually don't hatch.

If you discontinue watering but your lawn stays moist, try applying beneficial nematodes. These are microscopic worms that invade the bodies of the larvae and do them in. They don't harm people, beneficial insects, or worms. Nematodes are effective only if applied when soil temperatures are 55 degrees F or above. Since soil temperatures are too cold in spring, they are best applied in September. If you use nematodes, you have to keep the soil moist or the nematodes will die. They'll never eradicate the larvae, but they usually reduce numbers to levels that are not damaging.

Debug Turbo is an organic product containing neem and fatty oils. It's relatively safe for humans and should be applied according to label directions in spring. It also won't eradicate the larvae, but it should lower populations to undamaging numbers.

Resist the urge to apply chemical pesticides to control crane flies. There are a great number of beneficial creatures that help keep crane flies under control, and use of a nonselective pesticide will harm or kill many of the critters that help keep crane-fly populations low. Birds consider the larvae a gourmet treat. If you see a flock of starlings on your lawn, don't chase them away. Chances are they'll take care of the problem for you. Robins eat them as well. Adult crane flies are a favorite of birds and bats, and cat owners know what happens to any crane fly that suffers the misfortune of getting trapped in a home with a feline pet.

Perhaps the most interesting and entertaining predator of crane flies is the bald-faced hornet. These are the wasps that build huge paper nests in low-hanging trees, rhododendrons, and hedges. Unless the hornets have constructed their nest where it could present a hazard, resist the urge to spray it. These big black wasps with white spots on their heads and rumps are the eagles of the insect world. They rarely attack humans unless they think you are endangering their nests, and they consume all sorts of insects that harm our plants.

If you notice that you have bald-faced hornets flying around when the crane flies begin to emerge in summer, you may be in for an exciting show. The kids should enjoy it too. Lie on the grass and look for crane flies. The female hides in the grass. She's loaded with eggs and needs to lay them as soon as possible. Now look for a bald-faced hornet. She'll be hovering just above the grass hunting for a delicious meal. When the crane fly thinks the coast is clear, she'll beat her wings and take off clumsily into the air. If the hornet spots her, she swoops down on her and bites the crane fly's head off right in the air! All you hear is an "*Eek!*" and it's all over. The hornet bites off the crane fly's wings and legs, then carries her back to the hornet's nest for a barbecue.

The final message is that crane flies are rarely a big enough problem to warrant treatment. Take good care of your lawn, try not to let it get too wet, and invite birds and other beneficial critters into your garden.

Stick It to Flea Beetles

If you notice that something is chewing small round holes in the leaves of your vegetable crops, there's a good chance the insects doing the damage are flea beetles. They feed on the leaves of a wide variety of vegetable crops including beans, beets, most everything in the cabbage family, corn, mustard and other greens, eggplants, peppers, potatoes, tomatoes, and sweet potatoes. The adults chew small holes in leaves, while the larvae feed on roots.

Larval feeding rarely does serious harm, but in the case of potatoes, the grubs feed inside the tubers, creating a complex of winding grooves just below the surface of the skin, and leave entry holes into the potato filled with bug poop that looks like black gunk. Usually the potatoes are still edible, but with all of those tunnels and bug poop, they look less than appetizing.

Although flea beetles prefer vegetables, occasionally they'll take a liking to flowers, shrubs, and even trees. The worst damage occurs on young plants. Once a plant matures, the damage is usually only superficial, but young starts can be overrun and wiped out if flea-beetle populations are high.

There are a number of pesticides labeled to control flea beetles, but I don't recommend using them. They have to be used constantly to be effective and are harmful to beneficial insects, and most of them have health concerns associated with their use.

I learned of a great nonpesticide way to deal with flea beetles when, as a ten-year-old living in Wisconsin, I landed my first job as the lawn boy at a church near my home. One of my tasks was to help in the church garden, where caretaker Joe grew a wide variety of vegetables. Joe never used pesticides. Instead, he figured out all sorts of ingenious alternative methods to deal with pests. I still use many of the alternative methods I learned from Joe to manage pests in my garden today.

Flea beetles are so called because they have super strong back legs that allow them to jump like fleas, and they use them to escape at the first sign of trouble. That's one of the reasons they're so hard to control. If you walk up with a sprayer, they spring far from the plant the minute you begin the application.

Joe figured out how to use the insect's defense to our advantage. He cut out a 2-by-2-foot piece of plywood and painted heavy gear oil on one side, leaving a spot open on each side for me to hold it. He used gear oil because it was the only sticky material we had available. Now there's a product called Tanglefoot available at nurseries that is more effective and easier to work with.

Every morning, it was my job to take the board and sneak up to the plants holding the sticky side out. When I got right up to the plants I'd yell "Boo!" The beetles would leap for safety and get trapped on the sticky board.

Give this method a try and you'll become adept at catching them. You need to sneak up on them, sticky board in hand, only every other day for a week or two to solve the problem. There will always be a few escapees, but not enough to do serious harm. Even now, I find this task to be so much fun, I get bummed when I've wiped them out and I no longer need to sneak up on them.

One last tip: flea beetles often jump on gardeners to hitchhike to other plants. Change clothes before going to work in another garden, and especially before going home to work on your houseplants. If they get into your house, they'll riddle the leaves of your favorite plants. Even worse, it's practically impossible to convince visitors that the insects they see hopping off the couch aren't really fleas!

The Tempting Fruit

Nothing is more delicious than a crisp homegrown apple right off the tree. That is, unless the apple is infested with caterpillars and maggots. The only thing worse than biting into an apple to find half a caterpillar smiling back at you is to be greeted by the smiles of several half-eaten maggots. There are two pests that find their way into apples, and occasionally pears, in our area: codling moths and apple maggots.

Codling moths lay their eggs on twigs and, at times, on developing fruit. After hatching, the caterpillars bore into the apples or pears and tunnel to the core before heading out the other side, leaving a trail filled with reddish frass (polite word for bug poop). You can eat the fruit after cutting out the bad parts, but it won't keep well in storage.

Apple maggots, on the other hand, are fruit flies. The female lays several eggs directly into each fruit. After hatching, the maggots bore throughout the apple, creating irregular, winding tunnels that turn mushy brown, eventually rendering the fruit inedible. If you don't wait too long after harvest, the apples can be used in cooking, but don't tell your dinner guests that the pie has a little extra protein.

Over the years, experts have come up with quite a number of organic techniques to outwit these pests. I've tried every one of them but most methods have failed miserably. Many a year, my apples ended up a gourmet treat for my neighbor's horse.

The first method I tried to prevent apple maggots involved fake apples. I coated them with super sticky Tanglefoot, then hung them in the tree. The fruit fly thinks the fake is a real apple. When she lands on it to lay her eggs, she gets stuck.

The fake apples did a great job of catching the adult flies. The problem is that there are too many apple-maggot fruit flies out there. A friend of mine put five fake apples in her tree and kept track of how many fruit flies the apples caught in one season. Each fake apple caught about 5,000 fruit flies, yet every real apple on the tree was totally infested with maggots at harvest time.

There can be unforeseen consequences related to hanging sticky apples in your tree as well. One day, a woman from Chicago e-mailed me to ask if she could visit my garden while in Seattle on a business trip. I was happy to show her around. She had barely stepped out of her rental car when she reached out to admire a beautiful big apple she noticed on my tree. Unfortunately, it was one of those sticky fake apples and her hand stuck right to it. She couldn't get it off her hand—and it took quite an effort by both of us to get her free. By then we were both sticky messes, and she was so embarrassed she was several shades redder than the fake apple. I'm sure we both laugh remembering that day (actually, she might not laugh), but it was a pretty awkward way to meet someone for the first time.

The first method I tried to prevent codling moths was to wrap the trunk with corrugated cardboard, which I tied in place with garden twine. The caterpillars form cocoons in sheltered places, so the idea is to entice them to form cocoons under the cardboard. You need to periodically untie and remove it in order to put the el kabotski on the cocoons by squishing them. I found this task to be somewhat of a hassle, and regular removal, squishing, and retying didn't even put a dent in the number of apples infested with codling-moth caterpillars.

The next technique I tried was a nontoxic crop protectant, available online under the trade name Surround WP. This product is derived from kaolin clay, a material often used by potters. It has been proven to prevent both the caterpillars and the maggots from entering the fruit as long as you apply it every week, plus an additional application after every hard rain. It might have worked if I had managed to spray every week without fail. I only missed two or three of the weekly applications during the entire summer, but that's all it took. After all that work, my apples and pears ended up with just as many worms as if I hadn't sprayed.

Then I had a stroke of genius and came up with my own brilliant solution. I knew that in Japanese orchards, they put special bags over apples and pears to protect them from pests. After thinning the fruit, I tried covering each apple with a brown-paper lunch bag fastened to the stem with a bread tie. I should have listened to my wife when she told me she had serious doubts. I'll never know if my method would have actually prevented the worms from infesting the apples, because when it rained the bags got so heavy, they pulled all the apples off the tree!

Then a few years ago, someone discovered that covering individual fruit with pantyhose footies (marketed as apple-maggot barriers) is 100 percent effective against apple maggots. I definitely received strange looks from people walking by my house when they saw my tree filled with pantyhose footies. Although the footies helped to keep the apple maggots at bay, they proved to be less effective against codling moths, which were able to bore right through the material to gain entry to the fruit.

Now research from the University of Minnesota Extension has found that covering apples with zip-closure plastic sandwich bags is almost 100 percent effective at preventing both apple maggots and codling-moth larvae. Not only does this solution add even more plastic into the environment, it's just too much work. Putting a bag on each fruit can only be described as a Zen experience.

Recently City Fruit, a nonprofit organization in Seattle that assists homeowners in protecting and harvesting fruit in order to share it with food banks and other feeding programs, has been experimenting with covering entire trees with antihail netting. The netting is available online and at some local nurseries. According to Barb Burrill, orchard manager for City Fruit, when done correctly, covering fruit trees gives almost 100 percent control from fruit-infesting insects. There are obvious advantages to covering an entire tree, rather than individual fruits one at a time. Covering a tree is a bit of work, but after it's installed in early May, it protects the tree with no more labor until harvest time. Although the netting can be expensive, it's sturdy and can be reinstalled every spring for years.

There are a few challenges with covering a tree. First is determining how much netting to buy. City Fruit offers a handy calculator, online at CityFruit.org, to help figure out how much netting you need. Obviously the bigger the tree, the more material is needed and the more difficult it will be to cover the tree. A 5-foot-tall by 4-foot-wide tree requires a 15-foot-by-20-foot cover. The largest tree Barb recommends covering is 34 square feet, which requires a 26-foot-by-34-foot cover.

One problem is that shoots from the tree can grow through the netting. The shoots themselves are not a problem, but you will need to cut the shoots off when it's time to remove the cover. Problems can also occur if the cover is too tight against the branches. Anywhere the netting is pressed against the fruit, codling moths can bore right through it. An effective way to keep the netting away from the branches and fruit is to build a structure using bamboo poles capped with tennis balls. Zip-tie the bamboo poles into limbs within the tree so that the poles extend beyond the ends of the branches. Tying in bamboo poles actually makes net installation and removal easier, as the net slides over the tennis balls instead of snagging on the branches.

The net covers get dirty, so when you remove them at harvest time, wash them off with a hose and dry them thoroughly. Reusing a dirty cover could block light from reaching into the canopy to ripen your fruit.

It is advantageous to enlist a friend or two to help install the netting. The helpers can secure the two front corners with bamboo poles and use them to hoist the net over the top of the tree to drape down and cover all of the sides evenly. It may take five people to install the netting on a large tree. Secure the netting to the trunk of the tree with a soft tie like a rubber inner tube, and use twist ties to secure any spaces in the folds of the netting.

Even if your tree is too large to net completely, you can net individual branches by using the same bamboo-and–tennis ball structures and tying them in farther back on the limbs.

Finally, if covering your tree sounds like too much work, another option is to hire a tree service to install the netting. In Seattle, City Fruit offers a list of qualified tree services that install hail netting for a fee. Time will tell, but hopefully netting trees is the key to cooking apple pies without extra protein.

It's important to note that, before you install any barrier protection for your fruit, you'll want to thin the apples or pears. Thinning the fruit results in the same yield, but it comes in the form of fewer and substantially better-quality bigger fruit. Thinning also helps break the every-other-year pattern of production by reducing the energy drain that occurs when trees bear overly heavy crops. Thinning is effective only if you pull off the excess fruit before they exceed the size of a nickel. Thin apples and pears by removing all but the one largest fruit per cluster. I admit I always feel bad, yanking off and doing in all of those poor baby fruit, but I get over my guilt at harvest time. Get the thinning done early, and cover your trees with netting so you'll get to enjoy extra-big apples, without the extra protein.

Gentle Bees, Great Fruit

If the fruit on your tree doesn't tend to size up or falls off before it matures, the problem is most likely caused by a lack of pollination. European honeybee populations have been in serious decline over the last decade, and there just aren't enough of them left to get the job done. Fruit trees know they're on earth to reproduce and won't waste energy ripening fruit that doesn't develop seed. A pear is a good example. Each pear flower needs to be visited by a bee bearing pollen from the blossom of a different variety of pear at least thirty times in order to produce a pear that will mature on the tree.

Fortunately, it is possible to raise colonies of orchard mason bees (*Osmia lignaria*) in our own gardens to increase the size and quality of our fruit. Orchard mason bees are small blue native bees that are incredibly effective pollinators. You can purchase the bees in starter kits at quality nurseries during winter and usually at the Northwest Flower and Garden show.

Mason bees are better pollinators than European honeybees and fly in cooler weather. Unlike European honeybees, which travel a fairly long distance, visiting a limited number of flowers in each garden before heading back to the hive, mason bees venture only about 50 yards from their nesting sites, thereby allowing them to make hundreds of visits to flowers in your garden on a daily basis.

Another reason mason bees are such great pollinators is because they are clumsy fliers. Honeybees land gently, eat a little pollen, and collect some in their pouch before heading on to another flower. Mason bees fly like a B-29 bomber that has been hit by antiaircraft fire. They crash-land on a flower, sending pollen flying everywhere—including all over themselves. When they visit the next flower the same thing happens, and a tremendous amount of pollen gets transferred every time.

Blue mason bees are gentle creatures and almost never sting. At our house we often place a nesting block in the middle of our patio table so we can watch them bringing in pollen while we dine. Since all of the holes in a nesting block look the same, sometimes they get confused and go into the wrong house. It's hilarious to watch them backing out apologizing to the homeowner before heading into their own apartment.

I must, however, add one disclaimer about their ability to sting. A friend told me that he sat on one and found it to be a very uplifting experience!

Mason bees are solitary bees. They don't live in hives and they don't make honey. In nature these bees nest in all sorts of crevices such as hollow reeds or holes bored out by insects in the stems of plants. They also make their abodes in unexpected places. I've seen them nesting in piles of firewood and under slats on the side of a house. Therefore, if we want these bees to make our garden their home, we need to provide suitable nesting sites that mimic the ones they make use of in nature. This can include blocks of wood drilled with appropriate-size holes or special nesting trays filled with hollow cardboard tubes.

If you want to raise mason bees, it's best to begin with a starter kit containing bees to get the colony started. Starter kits come in all shapes and sizes, but all have 5/16-inch-diameter holes in wood blocks or cardboard tubes. Once you've got a colony started, you can make your own additional mason-bee blocks out of untreated wood. Drill appropriate-size holes lengthwise into the block of wood. The bees make chambers inside the nesting holes by constructing mud walls. They fill each chamber with pollen, lay an egg on it, and then seal the chamber shut with a mud partition.

Each mason-bee chamber is less than ½ inch wide; hence a single 12-inch-deep block of wood drilled with plenty of nesting holes can provide housing for an incredible number of bees. Remember that the back of the house needs to be solid, so don't drill all the way through the back of the wood block. If you accidentally drill all the way through, screw a board onto the back. Space the holes as evenly as you can, but don't worry if they aren't perfect. The blocks I drill generally end up looking like tenements, but the bees don't seem to mind. They prefer a clean house to fancy digs.

There are two serious problems that can harm mason bees and, if left untreated, wipe out entire colonies. Chalkbrood is a fungus that can spread inside the nesting blocks and kill bees on contact. Mites also accumulate on individual cocoons in nesting blocks, and emerging bees come out so covered with them, they can't even fly. If you use wood nesting blocks, you need to replace them at least every other spring to prevent a buildup of chalkbrood fungus and mites.

Unfortunately, the bees prefer the old blocks to the new ones and try to begin making new nests in them before you get a chance to remove them. There is a solution: As soon as it is evident that the bees are emerging in force, place a cardboard box over the blocks. The box must be located solidly against the wall that the nesting blocks are on so that the returning females can't enter through any gaps. Then cut a dime-size hole in the front of the box. The bees can see the light to find their way out, but can't find their way back in. As long as there are plenty of new nesting blocks available, the bees will begin making colonies in their new homes. Once all of the bees have vacated the used blocks, remove and soak them in a 10 percent bleach solution and then rinse out the holes with a powerful spray from the hose. Store the cleaned blocks and they'll be ready for use next spring.

The other option is to buy special nesting containers equipped with removable cardboard tubes. The tubes can be slit open during winter in order to remove and sterilize the cocoons by soaking them for a few minutes in a solution of 1 tablespoon bleach to 1 cup cold water. Dry the cocoons in a cool area and store them in a paper bag in the fridge until putting them outside in spring alongside new nesting tubes to allow the bees to make new colonies in them.

If all of this sounds like too much hassle, it is currently possible to rent orchard mason bee kits from RentMasonBees.com. Renting them is an easy and effective way to increase yields of fruit without having to care for the bees. Simply set up their nests in spring according to directions. You will need to return the kit in June and let the rental company do the work of cleaning and caring for the bees.

There are a couple of important things to be aware of if you decide to raise orchard mason bees. Keep a patch of moist clay-like soil in a location near the nesting site because they need mud to construct their chamber walls. Hang the nesting boxes outdoors on a sunny wall early enough in spring to give the bees time to warm up and emerge before the buds on fruit trees begin to bloom.

It's also wise to plant early-blooming shrubs and perennials to provide a food source nearby in case the bees emerge before the flower buds on fruiting plants open. One of the best shrubs to provide food for newly emerging mason bees is pieris, a member of the rhododendron family. When gardeners look at pieris, they see an elegant shrub with attractive little urn-shaped flowers in late winter through early spring. When the earliest-hatching mason bees look at pieris, they see Denny's! A single pieris is enough to feed hordes of hungry mason bees as they wait for the fruit trees to burst into bloom.

Finally, by June the nesting holes will be filled and all bee activity will cease. The adult bees live only four to six weeks and die by the end of May after the exhausting work of laying their eggs. In early June the larvae inside the chambers hatch and feed on the pollen in their mud-walled chambers for about ten days. The larvae then form cocoons and hibernate until they emerge as adults the following spring.

In early July it's a good idea to store the nesting blocks in a garage, shed, or basement for safe keeping during the summer and winter months. Yellow jackets and other predators occasionally work their way in to feed on the larvae. It will also keep the nesting blocks from getting too hot if they are located on a sunny wall. If you don't have anywhere to store them and the boxes are protected from hot afternoon sun, there usually is no real harm in leaving them outdoors year-round.

If you do leave the nesting blocks out during summer, don't panic (like I did) if you see woodpeckers sticking their long beaks into the holes to feast on your mason bees. When it happened to me, I called my good friend Brian Griffin, author of *The Orchard Mason Bee*, and told him that the birds were eating all my bees.

Brian told me I needn't worry—mama nature is too smart to let that happen. The bees lay the female eggs in the back of the block where the birds can't reach them. Us guys, on the other hand, are the sacrificial lambs. Our eggs are in the front of the block. Evidently we're just not as important in the scheme of things and they need far fewer of us.

One last warning: If you adopt mason bees, get ready to work hard during harvest time. Your well-pollinated fruit will become so big, it'll take three guys to bring each pear or apple into the house!

The Bald-Faced Truth

There are many kinds of wasps and most of them are considered to be beneficial. They parasitize and eat all sorts of harmful insects. Two varieties with bad reputations are yellow jackets and bald-faced hornets. Both of these kinds of wasps can give painful stings, but it should be noted that even these scary creatures can be highly beneficial insects as well, and most do much more good than harm.

Just for clarification purposes, it should be noted that bees and wasps are not the same. Both bees and wasps are capable of stinging, but a wasp can sting more than once, while a bee can sting only once and the act of stinging costs the bee its life. Wasps and bees look different as well. Wasps are smooth skinned and have the classic narrow wasp waist. Bees are hairier and plumper.

Most of the bigger wasps, such as yellow jackets and hornets, spend their time hunting or scavenging rather than visiting flowers. There are several different kinds of wasps that we call yellow jackets, and although some kinds can be troublemakers, especially when they bother our picnics, most rarely interact with humans unless they think their nest is under attack.

One of the most common types of yellow jackets is known as the paper wasp. This wasp is one of the most beneficial when it comes to helping control insect pests that attack our plants. Paper wasps build their nests under the eaves of your house. The nests, constructed of chewed bark, wood, and leaves mixed with saliva, resemble papier-mâché. They are filled with compartments where the wasps lay their eggs and rear their young. The nests start small but increase in size and can be nearly a foot in diameter by the end of summer. These lanky wasps are almost an inch long and have long legs that hang down when in flight. They fly high and rarely, if ever, bother humans. Instead, they search out caterpillars and other insects that tend to cause harm to our vegetables and ornamental plants. Once they capture their prey, they bring it back to the nest for a gourmet feast.

Despite the fact that paper wasps are highly beneficial, they are also quite capable of stinging. Sometimes they build their nest where opening a door could hit it or in high-traffic areas where there's risk of someone inadvertently disturbing it. In that case, it's usually necessary to spray in order to prevent danger to humans. If the nest is in a location where nobody will accidentally bump into it, simply leave it alone and let these beneficial critters do their work.

Much more troublesome to humans are the wasps commonly referred to as scavenger yellow jackets. These include the common yellow jacket, German yellow jacket, and, depending on the region where you live, the western or eastern yellow jacket. Although scavenger yellow jackets are mostly beneficial and capture and eat many harmful insects, they build up to incredibly high numbers by late summer, and they're the culprits that bother your picnic. Nothing can ruin a salmon barbecue faster than tons of these pesky insects crashing the party. They've been known to sting when people try to shoo them away and, much worse, these bothersome yellow jackets tend to enter pop cans unseen, making for some unpleasant surprises when unsuspecting picnickers take a drink.

People employ all sorts of methods to keep these pests away from their picnics, but yellow-jacket traps and the idea of hanging a salmon head over a pail of soapy water do little to dissuade the hordes of hungry wasps determined to compete for every bite.

Fortunately, there's a simple and effective way to repel these uninvited dinner guests.

Yellow jackets detest the odor of antistatic strips for the clothes dryer, and they almost always hit the road the minute they smell them. It has to be the stinky (a.k.a. fragrant) kind to work. If yellow-jacket pressure is low, a few of the strips hung over branches in nearby trees will do the trick. If multitudes of the little pests insist on sharing your dinner, put a few strips right on the table where you're eating. Tell the kids not to touch them, as they might contain chemicals that should not be handled at dinnertime.

These fragrant strips may repel a few of your invited guests along with the yellow jackets, but at least the diners who remain will get to enjoy their dinner without having to fend off yellow jackets for every bite.

Scavenger yellow jackets typically build their nests in the ground or inside structures, such as between the walls of a house or garage. Yellow jackets should never be allowed to nest inside the walls of your house. The wasps chew away at the wood and insulation and use it to build their nests between the wallboards. In areas with mild climates, colonies can exist between the walls for years; if you live where temperatures drop below freezing, the colony will die out in cold winter weather.

Even in areas with cold climates, however, new queens often find the entry hole the following spring and start a new colony next to the abandoned one. If this happens repeatedly over the years, the entire area between the walls of your house may be hollowed out. Even if you take action to eradicate the wasps between the walls, you'll need to make sure a queen won't return to start another colony again. Once you're sure they're gone in midwinter, find the entry hole and seal it up by filling it with wood putty.

By the way, never seal the entry hole in summer while the wasps have an active nest inside the walls. Even if you succeed without getting stung, once they realize they're trapped, the wasps will chew their way through the inner wall, and chances are they won't be in a good mood when they greet you in your living room.

Despite their bad manners and destruction to your home, even scavenger yellow jackets are beneficial. Like most large wasps, they eat all sorts of harmful insects. If the nest is located in an out-of-the-way location, the best policy might be to leave and let live.

Unfortunately, yellow jackets can be very aggressive if anyone comes too close to their nest. If the nest is located inside the walls of the house, or if a ground nest is in a place where it could present a danger to pets or humans, you should take action to spray it.

Among the most beneficial of all wasps, and also most feared by people, are the bald-faced hornets. Technically yellow jackets, these big wasps can grow to almost an inch long. They're shaped like yellow jackets, but instead of yellow stripes, they have a white spot on their head and white stripes on their abdomen.

These are the wasps that build the volleyball-size paper nests in trees and shrubs. It's understandable why we fear them. They're armed with powerful venom and are capable of stinging over and over again. Anyone who has ever accidentally run into one of their nests will never forget the experience. Fortunately, bald-faced hornets rarely sting away from their nests and almost never bother picnics. Instead they are incredibly effective hunters and spend their time searching out many of the bugs that harm our gardens and bring them back to the nest to feed the colony.

Obviously, having these intrepid hunters devouring harmful bugs in our gardens is to our advantage. If you find a nest where it doesn't present a threat to kids or pets, allow it to remain. Put up warning signs and barricades to prevent accidental contact with the nest. Then give the kids a thorough safety talk before inviting them to watch the wasps in action from a safe distance. They'll learn about nature as they watch the workers expand the size of the nest with papier-mâché chewed from wooden structures and tree bark. Most fun of all, they'll get to observe hornets bringing crane-fly larvae, caterpillars, aphids, and a wide assortment of other garden pests into the nest destined for a delicious evening meal.

Whether you have paper wasps, scavenger yellow jackets, or bald-faced hornets, you may need to destroy their nest if people or pets are in danger of running into them. You always want to spray out a scavenger yellow jacket nest that is in the walls of your house.

You can hire a professional to do the job. Only do it yourself if you aren't allergic to stings, and do it at night. Use an aerosol spray that freezes them on contact in case they swarm. Wear lots of clothing, button up, and wear rubber bands around shirtsleeves and pant cuffs to make sure the wasps cannot get inside your clothes. Wear goggles, as wasps go for the eyes.

Most important, when dealing with wasps at night: don't hold the flashlight. Use a flashlight, but put it on a chair so that you can illuminate the target without carrying it. Yellow jackets are attracted to the light, and if anything goes wrong and you run away with a flashlight in your hand, it will serve as a beacon telling the wasps "Hey, guys, here I am—come get me!"

Most people know little about the benefits of yellow jackets and hornets and see them only as dangerous pests. Not surprisingly, then, most nests, even those of bald-faced hornets, are sprayed as soon as they're found, even if they are located where they present little or no threat to humans and pets. That was the policy when I began working at Seattle University in 1978. All hornet nests discovered on campus had to be sprayed, *no exceptions*.

I was uncomfortable killing such beneficial creatures, especially when they were located in back areas of the campus where they didn't present a safety hazard, yet I went along with the policy.

That all changed after I was forced to spray a nest on the side of a building. My boss called me and said that hornets had somehow built a nest right in the middle of a window, outside an administrator's office. The office was on the fourth floor, and although no one ever opened the windows in that office, just seeing them there made the administrator uneasy and he insisted on its removal.

I came in to do the job at night. Since it was apparent that I would have to climb out an adjacent window and stand on a ledge, my future wife came along to help. It was her job to shut the window, preferably after I climbed back in, if anything went wrong and the wasps swarmed.

I managed to spray the nest without getting stung, but seeing hundreds of dying hornets stagger out before falling from the nest really bummed me out. Then, to add to my misery, while walking across campus the next day, I ran into my fellow gardener, José, who was from Brazil. When I told him what I had done, he looked horrified and told me that, according to Brazilian folklore, spraying a wasp nest brings five years of bad luck!

I was so upset after that incident, I requested a meeting and somehow persuaded the powers that be to agree to a new policy. From that time on, only nests located where they presented a risk to public safety had to be eradicated. Nests located in back areas of the campus were allowed to remain. The only requirement was that I had to cordon off the area with caution tape and put up signs to warn off anyone who might accidentally stray into the area.

The new policy worked great for the first couple of years. The hornets cooperated by building their nests only in back areas. I often observed bald-faced hornets busily hunting for insect pests, playing a key role in our campus biological pest-control program. Then one year I received the dreaded call from my boss: Two good-size hornet nests had been discovered right in the heart of the campus. He expected me to keep my end of the bargain and spray out both of them.

At first I agreed to do it, but then I came up with a brilliant idea. Rather than spray them, I decided to move the nests to a back area where they were allowed. My boss thought I was out of my mind, but as long as I promised to do it right away, and in the middle of the night, he reluctantly agreed to let me try. I readied a couple of good relocation areas with signs and caution tape.

Luckily a beekeeper friend was able to loan me a bee suit. My friend warned me to wear heavy clothing under the bee suit, because it might not be thick enough to protect against hornet stings. Even more disconcerting, he warned me that I needed to wear goggles as well. Evidently hornets are capable of shooting venom into your eyes through the face netting!

I arrived at the campus at two in the morning. I quickly suited up, and considering that the bee suit was about twice my size and the only eye protection I could find was a spray mask that covered half my face, I'm sure I looked like some kind of alien being. On my way across campus, I ran into a security guard. At first he offered to help me, but when he learned what I was about to do, he suddenly remembered he had to check the garage for parking violations.

I decided to take on the biggest nest first. It was about the size of a soccer ball and was constructed around a good-size branch in a rhododendron. My plan was to first insert the nest and the branch it was on into a large clear-plastic bag, then cut off the branch once it was inside the bag. With the nest sealed in the bag, I'd transport it to the prepared back area. I would then take the nest out of the bag and lay it into my preselected bush.

Before moving in on the nest, I set the flashlight on a nearby bench with the beam shining directly on the nest. The first thing I noticed were two huge hornets guarding the entryway. They seemed to be saying, "Hey, buddy, what do you think you're going to do?"

I was a nervous wreck, but I finally gathered my courage and put the bag over the nest and the branch it was on, then cut the branch off of the shrub. I don't recall what I thought would happen, but it wasn't what I expected. The bald-faced hornets came roaring out of the nest like Pickett's Charge. The whirlwind of angry wasps caused the bag to heave and undulate so wildly, I almost lost hold of it. It was so difficult to control, it practically knocked me over, but I somehow managed to lug it over to the designated location on the other end of campus.

That's when I suddenly realized that I had to let them out of the bag! I waited about ten minutes, hoping the hornets would calm down. They didn't. Finally I took a deep breath, opened the bag, and pulled out the branch with the nest.

Despite wasps swarming around, I managed to wedge the nest into the rhododendron bush I had designated for this purpose. I suspected that if the nest fell out of the shrub and ended up on the ground, the wasps would desert it and most likely try to rebuild it somewhere else on campus. To my great relief, cradled by the branches, the nest stayed in the rhododendron.

By now the wasps were all over me. I turned to run, but I noticed that when I dropped the plastic bag, the open ends sealed together, thereby trapping hundreds of bald-faced hornets inside. I grabbed the back of the bag and took off running.

So there I was, an alien being in an ill-fitting white suit, running across campus holding a plastic bag with hundreds of wasps streaming out of the back, when I practically ran into an inebriated man holding a bottle of fortified wine. He dropped the bottle and ran screaming and I never saw him again. To this day, I don't know if I killed him or cured him.

After going through all of that, I wasn't too excited about taking on a second nest. I courageously overcame my terror and forced myself to tackle the job. Unfortunately this time, when I tried to place the nest into the designated shrub, it fell out of the branches and landed on the ground. I tried to pick it up and place it back in the bush, but there were so many hornets all over me, I chickened out and ran. As I feared, the hornets deserted the nest and tried to rebuild it close to where it had been before in the heart of campus. I suspect it was a janitor that sprayed and put an end to it before it ever gained much size.

At least I didn't have the curse of *another* five years' bad luck hanging over me.

The other nest, the one that remained in the shrub, ended up a huge success. The hornets increased the size of the nest, encompassing several of the closest branches in the process. All summer long I watched hornets bringing caterpillars, larvae, and other insect pests kicking and screaming into the nest to be served up as a gourmet treat for the colony. It gave me a great feeling to know that I had helped save the lives of all of those beneficial creatures. Just don't ask me to do it again!

PART 4

Seattle University, Never a Dull Moment

Don't Make a Political Statement with Horse Manure

For a short time I used composted horse manure as a mulch in the garden beds at Seattle University. I learned about it from a woman who attended one of my garden talks. She owned a stable where they boarded a lot of horses and asked me if I ever used horse manure in the garden. I didn't know anything about the qualities of horse manure, but she assured me that she used it with great success in her own garden.

The woman told me that horse manure is high in plant nutrients; plus the wood shavings used for bedding breaks down to form outstanding topsoil. She did warn me, however, that the manure must be well composted or it can cause problems. If it's too fresh, high amounts of ammonia and salts could possibly burn roots and interfere with seed germination.

Another problem is that horses eat a lot of weeds. Weeds are not a problem with cow manure because cows have four stomachs to help break down everything, including the weed seeds. Horses have only one stomach, which doesn't do a good job of breaking down the seeds. If it isn't well composted, horse manure can definitely cause a weed problem. Of course, uncomposted horse manure can be quite odiferous as well.

When she cleaned out the stables, the horse manure and bedding was stored in a long row far from the stable. When the pile got too big, she would have some hauled away. The manure usually sat there for about four months, so as long as we collected the manure from the oldest section, we could count on its being well composted. She was happy to give it away and offered that we could come anytime and take as much as we wanted.

The stable was near Bridle Trails State Park, only about a forty-minute drive from Seattle University, so I decided to send a couple of gardeners over to collect some to test using it on a few select gardens. After applying the manure as mulch in the test gardens, I was sold on the idea. The plants where we used it were thriving, and we didn't notice excessive weeds or odor. Best of all, it was free for the taking. We began using it on a regular basis.

Then disaster struck. Unbeknownst to me, there had been a major rainstorm in the vicinity of the stable. The deluge dumped an unusually heavy amount of rain, and the manure pile, which was quite large at the time, acted as a dam, forming a good-size lake behind it. Unfortunately, the dam gave way and the neighbors downhill from the stables ended up with basements flooded with manure tea. The regional Environmental Protection Agency was called in, and the stable was no longer allowed to store large amounts of manure on-site. From that time on, it had to be collected on a biweekly basis.

Knowing nothing about this, I sent our two seasonal gardeners out to collect manure. Seasonal gardeners were hired for the summer months to help with less-skilled tasks and weren't expected to have great gardening skills. They didn't realize that the exceptionally pungent pile of manure had been swept from the stables only the day before and was too new to use. Worse yet, they followed my instructions to a tee and spread the manure right in front of the Administration Building on an 86-degree F day.

I knew something was wrong when my office phone started ringing off the hook. I picked it up, and the administrative assistant from the president's office was sputtering and stammering so loudly I could barely catch what he was saying.

I headed over to see what was going on. I was still a couple of blocks away from the Administration Building when I got my first whiff of a very unpleasant farmyard odor. Then when I arrived there, the first thing I saw was the whole front side of the building covered in flies. I'm a firm believer in the old saying that a coward dies many times in battle, while the valiant only once, but I turned tail and ran back to my office. I had the definite feeling it would be wiser to give tempers time to cool before dealing with the big shots about this problem.

As it turned out, I decided to leave the horse manure in place. It had already done its damage by burning the tweetle out of shallow-rooted shrubs and perennials. Trying to remove it would be difficult and most likely would mix the weed seeds into the soil, making them more likely to germinate all at once.

Despite the fact that we watered heavily and often to help the odor dissipate, the essence of Iowa persisted for about four days. The story made the school paper and was a big hit with the students, who thought it was hilarious. Eventually most of the top brass saw the humor in it as well, although there are still a few who are convinced to this day that I was making a political statement about their administrative abilities!

Just remember that when it comes to using any kind of manure in your garden, make sure that it is well composted. Typically if you just let the pile sit, it usually takes three to four months for the manure to break down to usable compost. You can speed up the process if you turn the pile over; use a pitchfork on a small pile or if you're storing lots of it, use a tractor equipped with a front loader. The best way to know when manure is mature enough to use is by checking the compost itself to see if it is ready. If the manure is well composted, it will look like soil and will have lost its manure smell. Once that happens you can feel confident that the manure you're spreading will benefit your plants and soil, and you won't be forced to throw a wine party to repair relationships with your closest neighbors.

Oak Tree Saga

The Seattle University campus has long been famous for its collection of specimen trees. Among the most majestic are a couple of huge red oaks (*Quercus rubra*) located at the top of a steep bank across from the Administration Building, right in the heart of campus. No one knows for sure how they got there or who planted them, but their 80-foot-tall-by-60-foot-wide canopy dominates the north-campus skyline, especially in fall when the leaves turn spectacular shades of red and scarlet.

There used to be three of these magnificent trees growing in that area. Not long after I was hired as director for grounds care on the campus, I noticed a problem that could have put an end to all three of them. One of the trees wasn't faring well. The leaves were stunted, and there was a lot of dieback in the canopy. I suspected that the tree was under attack by a fungus called Armillaria root rot, which is known to infect more than twenty-five species of ornamental trees and shrubs and is exceptionally deadly to oak trees.

Upon inspection, I discovered a number of telltale symptoms. There were honey-colored mushrooms growing in clusters near the base of the tree, with caps 1 inch high and 2 to 4 inches wide. Under the bark there were root-like black strands attached to the larger roots, and lighter fan-shaped mats of fungal strands were also apparent. There was no doubt that the tree was seriously infected with Armillaria root rot.

The disease spreads primarily by root-like fungal strands that grow from infected plants through the soil to adhere to the roots of nearby plants. Fortunately, although the other two red oaks were only a couple of hundred feet from the affected tree, the fungal strands had not yet spread that far. I had to take immediate action, however, to prevent the disease from infecting the other two red oaks.

There are no chemicals that will control Armillaria. The only effective way to prevent it from spreading is to remove the infected plant material. That meant removing the tree and digging out the stump and as many of the roots as possible. Removing the infected parts, however, was not a simple undertaking by any means. The tree had a trunk measuring over 6 feet wide at the base. Worst of all, budget restraints made it necessary that we take on the job in-house.

We first had to climb the tree with safety ropes in order to cut and lower all of the limbs and branches. Once that huge task was completed, we were left with an enormous 15-foot-tall stump to deal with. Since the tree was growing at the top of a steep incline above a grassy field, we decided it was safest to cut it off near the base and let the entire stump fall down the bank. We could then use our backhoe to dig out the gigantic stump and as many of the roots as possible.

When you chop down a large tree stump with a chain saw, you want to make an undercut opposite the point where you will begin sawing. Start by figuring out where you want the tree to fall and make the undercut facing that direction. The top of the undercut should be at about a 60-degree angle, sawing to a depth of 20–25 percent of the tree's diameter. Complete the undercut by making a horizontal cut that meets the lower end of the top cut. If all goes well, the tree should hinge and fall in the desired direction.

The only problem was that a beautiful ornamental cherry tree was growing on the bank about 12 feet directly below the stump. The oak was leaning to the side, however, so as long as the undercut was made correctly, the tree would fall on a trajectory that wouldn't flatten the cherry.

Although I was a certified arborist, I decided that the stump would make a great training aid for DC, our recently hired senior gardener. DC was a very skilled gardener but wasn't used to dealing with chain saws. Unfortunately, after DC made the undercut, I could tell it wasn't located correctly and I was sure the tree would hit the cherry. DC, however, was adamant that the undercut was just right and the tree would miss it.

We decided to make a high-stakes bet on the outcome. If the trunk flattened the cherry, DC had to give me an extra-large peanut butter chocolate chip cookie. If the stump missed it, I had to buy him the cookie.

Despite the undercut, the huge trunk was still totally secure, so we decided to take a coffee break before making the big cut to see who won. We had a lot of student help on our grounds crew, and word quickly spread around campus that we were going to fell the big trunk and had a bet on the outcome. When we came back to finish the job, there were close to a hundred students and faculty there to watch the tree felling and to see who would win.

Everyone in the crowd was shouting encouragement as DC cranked up the chain saw. It seemed to take forever, but finally the saw cut through to the undercut. For a moment the giant trunk teetered on its axis, then pivoted and started to fall right toward the cherry tree. Events seemed to happen in slow motion. Everyone held their breath as the huge log headed downward on its route of destruction. Just as it was about to crush the tree, the top of the trunk hit a rise on the steep bank and, to everyone's amazement, the gigantic trunk bounced over the cherry without touching it. A huge cheer erupted from the crowd.

And as you may have already guessed, I had to give DC the cookie!

Oak Tree Saga . . . Continued

The saga of the oak tree didn't quite end with cutting it down. We still had to dig out and dispose of an enormous 3-foot-tall stump and root system. In those days we had a backhoe equipped with a digging bucket and a front loader that we used for all sorts of landscaping projects. I love the living tweetle out of running backhoes, but DC (the cookie winner) was the regular backhoe operator and, therefore, more practiced. I got to run it now and then because I was the boss.

As it turned out, soon after we cut down the tree, DC went on vacation. Since it was imperative to get the roots out right away, I eagerly took control of the backhoe to dig out the stump.

The stump was so big, it took practically an entire day to dig it out. When I finally managed to get the stump and its root-ball out of the hole, it was so heavy the front loader couldn't lift it. The stump was way too massive to place in the bed of our work trucks anyway. I decided the best way to dispose of it was to put it in the campus dumpster. The dumpster was located across campus at the bottom of a steep ramp, about 12 feet below a platform where we would back up our work trucks to dump brush and debris into it. I decided to use the front loader to roll the stump there. That meant rolling it right through the heart of campus, where it would make an incredibly muddy mess on the thoroughfares that students and faculty use to get to class. I knew my grounds crew could get the mud cleaned up quickly. My real concern was what might happen when I dropped the stump into the dumpster.

When I finally got the stump to the loading dock, I was dismayed to see that the dumpster was empty. I was hoping there would be debris to cushion the blow when I dropped it in. I couldn't think of any alternative way to dispose of the stump, however. I decided to go for it. It was so heavy, I could barely get the front loader to lift it over the 1-foot-tall lip at the edge of the loading dock. Suddenly there was a feeling of weightlessness and I realized the stump was airborne.

It landed with a deafening roar. When the dumpster finally stopped bouncing, I noticed that its sides were bowed out from the width of the stump. Fortunately the dumpster seemed intact, so I figured I hadn't harmed it enough to worry about. Relieved to have all of that over with, I called the disposal company to have the dumpster picked up that night. I thought I was home free.

I knew I was wrong when I saw the look on my boss's face the next day. The owner of the disposal company had called him first thing that morning. As he told it, when the truck came to pick up the dumpster, it was so heavy the pulling mechanism could barely yank the dumpster onto the truck bed. Then the truck overheated while driving to the top of the ramp, and the driver had to change his route in order to avoid any steep hills on his way to the landfill. Then, when the driver raised the truck bed to empty the dumpster at the landfill, the stump was wedged in and wouldn't budge until the bed was raised to its highest level. When the stump finally broke free, it took the doors at the end of the dumpster along with it!

The university was not only stuck with a costly bill for repair of the dumpster, the disposal company threatened to drop us as clients unless we guaranteed nothing similar would ever happen again. What really made my boss mad was that the university was self-insured and, since my grounds budget was basically spent for the year, the cost of the dumpster repair ended up coming out of *his* budget!

If I had to remove a huge stump again, I'd rent the biggest chain saw I could find to cut the stump into pieces before disposing of it. As a homeowner, I'd hire a tree service to chop it up and take it away.

If you ever discover Armillaria in your garden, after digging out the infected tree and as many roots as possible, take the additional steps I did to prevent it from spreading to other susceptible trees in the vicinity. Start by watering carefully. Drought-stressed trees are much more susceptible to infection, as are trees sitting in constantly wet soil. Water deeply and infrequently, and dig into the soil from time to time to check that there is adequate moisture in the root zone. Mulch over the soil surface with arborist's wood chips. Wood-chip mulch has been found to greatly increase the beneficial fungi that make soil nutrients more available to woody plants. The chips also encourage beneficial microbes that help suppress soil-borne diseases and harmful fungi such as Armillaria.

I'm happy to report the two other red oaks remain disease-free to this day and are among the most beautiful and majestic trees on the Seattle University campus. I'm also happy to report that my boss didn't fire me for throwing the stump in the dumpster, and I continued working at Seattle University for another twenty-three years.

Colorado Blue Spruce Belongs in Colorado

When I began working at Seattle University in 1978, one of the first things I discovered was that there were a lot of Colorado blue spruce trees (*Picea pungens glauca*) on the campus. In the right climate, these can be beautiful trees. Most have the classic Christmas-tree shape and feature sky-blue foliage.

The problem is that in areas with mild climates, such as the west side of the Cascade Range, from Northern California up into British Columbia, these trees are highly susceptible to small green insects known as spruce aphids. These nasty critters attack in the middle of winter, sometimes as early as Christmas. By the time the damage is noticed in spring, it's too late. The aphids suck the juice out of the needles, causing them to dry up and drop off. Serious infestation often results in unsightly denuded trees with foliage remaining only at the end of the branches.

The odd thing about spruce aphids is that they don't show up in damaging numbers every year. Although small numbers of the aphids are usually present in any given winter, injurious populations usually occur only every few years. Damage can take place two or three years in a row, but then the aphids might not show up in large numbers again for another five or six years.

There are two ways that you can deal with spruce aphids and keep spruce trees looking attractive. The first is to spray the trees on a yearly basis in late January. The other method is to monitor the trees and only treat if the aphids are present in damaging numbers.

Before I began at the university, the gardeners had been using the yearly spray approach. It kept the trees looking attractive, but there were obvious downsides to the practice. First, there are health and environmental concerns associated with spraying chemical pesticides on a yearly basis. The annual spray program also resulted in a waste of money and labor, since in most years there wouldn't have been enough aphids present to do noticeable harm. Needless to say, it was time for a new strategy when it came to dealing with spruce aphids, and as the new director for grounds and landscaping, I had to come up with it.

I immediately set up a monitoring system so that any spraying would be done only if aphids were actually present in damaging numbers. I began monitoring in late December and repeated the process every two weeks until mid-February. To monitor for aphids, ask a helper to hold a manila file folder under some of the older growth in the lower branches of the tree (spruce aphids generally show up in the lower branches first). Wearing gloves, hold the end of the branch with one hand and use the flat of your other hand to gently whack the living tweetle out of the branch above the file folder. Sift through the needles that drop onto the folder to look for little green aphids hiding in the duff. If you find fewer than eight aphids per sample, no treatment is needed at that time. If you find more than eight aphids per sample, it's time to take action.

My first year at Seattle U turned out to be a bad one for spruce aphids. While monitoring I found ten to fifteen aphids per sample, and I knew I had to act. At the same time, I was determined to find a nonchemical treatment that would kill the aphids without endangering health or harming the environment.

There was another concern as well. The most beautiful Colorado blue spruce on the campus was (and still is) planted in a Japanese garden above a waterfall that spills down into a pond below, and the pond contained fish. Every year, when the gardeners sprayed the spruce, pesticides dripped into the pond and inevitably killed the fish. The yearly fish kills were highly unpopular with the student community, but the gardeners felt they had to do it to save the spruce tree. I was determined to find a way to deal with the aphids without harming the fish.

My first idea was to use soap. I had learned to use Ivory soap to control aphids while working as an assistant gardener at a neighborhood church when I was a kid in Wisconsin.

When I went to buy it, however, I learned that Ivory soap was a thing of the past. All I could find was Ivory detergent, and I was unsure whether it might harm plants. I did a test spray on a few of the campus birch trees, before trying it on the spruces. It did a pretty good job of controlling the aphids, but I learned an important lesson: if you spray detergent in a power sprayer, don't forget to use an antisudsing agent. There were so many bubbles in the trees, it looked like Lawrence Welk had spent the afternoon on campus.

One other problem with Ivory detergent: State law requires anyone with a pesticide applicator license to apply only sprays that are labeled for use as pesticides by the state Department of Agriculture. Because I was certified, I could not legally use Ivory detergent. Fortunately I found Safer brand insecticidal soap that was labeled for this purpose. Pesticidal soap is specially made to kill soft-bodied insects, such as aphids, and is safe for the environment, people, and pets.

I wasn't at all sure it would work, but I bought a case of the soap and prepared to give it a try on the campus spruces.

The big experiment was undertaken early in the morning at the start of January. It turned out to be a big waste of time—soap kills the aphids only if you hit them directly. It works quite well on plants you can get close to and thereby spray both sides of the leaves, but on tall spruce trees with aphids hiding on all of those needles, it failed to hit many of them and didn't do much good at all.

Even worse, to my surprise and horror, the soap killed the fish in the Japanese garden. They were clean, but they were dead! The students were upset and there was even an article in the school newspaper calling me a fish murderer. After that disaster, I gave up and didn't spray the spruces again that year. Many of them dropped needles and ended up looking pretty bad. Some of the administrators weren't happy with me. I knew I'd better come up with a better strategy by the following year, or I might be looking for a new job.

The following summer I did quite a bit of research to find a safe, environmentally friendly spray that would do in the aphids without murdering the fish. By luck, I happened across an article mentioning that horticultural oils are sometimes used to control spruce aphid. Horticultural oils, available at most garden centers, are highly refined from petroleum. They're effective against a wide variety of insects, yet cause little harm to the environment and are safe for humans and pets.

The downside is that horticultural oil will kill any beneficial insect it hits, but since sprays for spruce aphid are applied in winter, there are few, if any, beneficial insects present. The one major concern I had was the warning label that stated oil sprays can kill fish.

When I monitored the following December, my samples found record numbers of aphids. I couldn't risk another damaging year, so I decided to apply the oil spray, despite misgivings about what it might do to the fish in the pond.

Again, I sprayed in the early morning. When I went to check the next day, there was good news and bad news. The spray was extremely effective and knocked the aphid population down well below damaging numbers. The bad news was that, for some reason, the oil spray turned the trees from their normal beautiful blue to an ugly dull green.

I could only imagine the looks on the administrators' faces when they saw the blue spruce had turned olive. By pure luck, however, when the new growth occurred in early spring, the sparkling blue needles contrasted beautifully against the background of dull green, making the trees look the best they had in years. I, of course, took full credit for the whole effect.

In case you're wondering, the fish weren't harmed in the least and I was elevated to hero status among a good portion of the student population. Be aware that spraying oil near a water feature *might* kill the fish in it. The label warns that it could, so if you try it, know that you're taking a risk. I will say, however, that I sprayed that spruce in the Japanese garden with horticultural oil several times in subsequent years, and I kept my hero status; I never again harmed the fish.

Hitchhike a Ride with a Tow Truck

When I began working at Seattle University in 1978, there wasn't much of a grounds-care budget and it would be another year before we could buy our own backhoe. So when my boss called me to tell me that they were putting in a ramp for disabled access in front of Bellarmine Hall, one of the campus dormitories, I was concerned. There was a spectacular tree growing right where the ramp was going in.

The tree was a magnificent upright red-leaved Japanese maple that had been brought to the campus by the famous Japanese landscaper Fujitaro Kubota. Starting in the late '40s, Kubota did much of the landscaping at Seattle University, and he hand-picked spectacular trees for the campus. Judging from its size, I figured the tree must be about a hundred years old. The only way I could save this beautiful specimen was to dig it up and move it.

The construction project was scheduled to begin in two weeks. In order to move a tree of this size, I needed a backhoe. The canopy of the tree was about 25 feet tall and 15 feet wide, and the diameter of the trunk at the base of the tree was about 8 inches wide.

When transplanting a tree, the rule of thumb is to provide 10 to 12 inches of root-ball for every inch of trunk diameter at ground level. That meant digging at least a 6-foot-wide root-ball. Unfortunately, I'd already overspent my budget for the year and there wasn't any money left over to rent a backhoe. When I asked my boss to rent one for me, he said his budget was strained to the limit as well. I'd have to figure out some other way to move the tree.

There was no alternative but to dig it out by hand. In those days we relied heavily on student labor, and I assigned six of the student grounds employees to help dig out the tree. We began by digging a wide trench around the trunk until we reached the bottom of the root-ball. We then dug under the ball, cutting roots until we could rock the tree enough to tell if the root-ball was free. Any roots damaged in the digging process were cut cleanly to prevent damaged root ends from becoming diseased. It took about a week of full-time hard digging, but we got it done.

Now the problem was figuring out how to get the tree out of the hole. We carved down one side of the hole to form a ramp and covered it with a big plywood board to facilitate pulling the tree out of the hole. Then we wrapped ropes around the root-ball and tied them to our biggest truck. When I gunned the engine, the wheels just spun on the blacktop. The tree didn't budge.

I was stymied. Even if I could find a way to get the tree out of the hole, I couldn't think of a way to move it all the way across campus to its designated location.

By pure luck, right at that moment, a tow truck drove by towing a car that had been illegally parked on the campus. The thought suddenly came to me that tow trucks are equipped with big cranes. I figured if they're powerful enough to pick up the front of a good-size car, they might just be capable of lifting a good-size tree.

I ran swiftly after the truck and caught the driver's attention before he drove off. I asked him how much it would cost to tow a tree across campus. After I convinced him I wasn't joking, he called in to his headquarters and they gave him permission to come back and give it a try. The charge would be $40, a bargain even in 1978.

There was easy access and the tow truck was able to back right up to the tree. Since the truck was using a crane, the first step was to wrap the trunk with a special nylon strap made to lift trees by the trunk. The strap is equipped with eye couplets, and the hook on the crane was inserted into the couplets for lifting. The strap must be wrapped tightly around the trunk, making sure there are no twists or slack. Any slippage that occurs while lifting can cause serious injury to the tree by tearing the bark. I was also worried that branches might break if the tree began to rotate as it was lifted, so as a last step before trying the crane, we pulled the tree over on its side so that the student gardeners could hold on to the upper branches to prevent the tree from spinning as the root-ball was raised.

We held our breath when the driver engaged the crane. It strained under the weight, and the back of the truck dipped ominously. Then, all of a sudden, the root-ball rose from the hole. We all started to cheer.

As the tree rose, however, the weight of the root-ball made the tree go vertical. The top shot upward, taking a few of the students with it, leaving them dangling 20 feet up in the air!

The quick-thinking tow-truck driver lowered the root-ball to the ground, bringing the top down to where the students could drop off safely. Before lifting it again, we tied ropes to the branches and used them to control swaying. (Why didn't I think of that in the first place?)

Moving very slowly, the tow truck managed to carry the tree the four blocks across campus to a previously prepared planting hole on the south side of Xavier Hall. The tree not only survived the tow-truck transplant, but thrived in its new location. To this day, it's one of the prized Japanese maples on the campus.

So if you ever need to move a good-size tree a short distance, using a tow truck might be a viable alternative. Just don't ask your helpers to hold on to the upper branches!

I Never 'Fessed Up . . . and Never Will

I've always loved trying to figure out ingenious ways to solve the most vexing problems in the garden. One problem I had at Seattle University—but it could just as easily have occurred in a home garden—involved moving a huge rock that was in the wrong place.

Years ago, no one knows when or why, someone stuck a big rock out in the middle of a lawn. The rock created a maintenance nightmare because it was situated near enough to a tree that it made it impossible to get the riding lawn mower between the tree and the rock. That left a single strip of grass requiring a special trip with a hand mower every time we cut the grass.

Even worse, tall grass grew up around the rock where the mower wasn't able to get close enough to cut it. We didn't use herbicides such as Roundup at the university, so the gardener who cared for that area of the campus was forced to power trim around the rock at least once per week to keep it from looking unsightly. Our garden crew was understaffed, and we weren't keeping up with the mowing and trimming very well. I was receiving a lot of complaints about the situation from the administration and knew I had to come up with a solution.

I thought about removing the grass and putting a garden between the rock and the tree, but it just wasn't the right place for a garden. The only solution I could come up with was to move the rock.

I like to incorporate rock into gardens, so I was happy to have the big rock at my disposal. Moving the rock, however, wasn't an easy task.

First of all, this rock was big. It looked like it weighed about a ton. The other problem was that my budget was stretched to the limit. We still didn't have a backhoe at SU, and renting one was expensive. I couldn't afford the cost without sacrificing a bunch of cool perennials I was planning to buy for a new planting on the other side of the campus.

Another problem was that the rock was located where access was difficult. The lawn surrounding the rock was constantly wet, because it was at the bottom of a hill and collected runoff from the upper campus. My first thought was to hire a tow truck to pick up the rock (I had done this years before to move a Japanese maple). The lawn was so muddy around the rock, however, that even if I put plywood down to drive on, I might still sink the tow truck up to its axles. Then I really would have a problem.

My next plan was to tie a metal cable to the rock and attach it to our biggest truck. I dug around the rock until I could get a chain around it, then hooked the cable to our heaviest pickup truck. When I throttled full blast, I practically burned off the tires. The rock didn't even budge.

That's when I thought of our come-along. A come-along is a portable winch with a cable and a lever arm. Its gears allow a relatively light force on the lever to pull heavy items attached to a cable. The one we had purchased was a super-heavy-duty model rated to pull loads as heavy as 2 tons. We had bought it two years earlier to remove a huge tree stump that we had dug out. It was the only time that we had used it, but it worked well. You need to attach the come-along to something strong and stable to winch from. There was a large tree near the stump we'd had to remove, so we'd attached the come-along to the tree's trunk after covering it with rubber to keep the bark unharmed. It enabled us to pull the stump out by hand in an area where we couldn't use heavy equipment. I knew that we would also be able to move the rock with the come-along.

I came in early the next day to move the rock, as I didn't want people around in case the cable broke and went flying. The problem was that I couldn't find anything to hook the come-along to. I didn't think the brakes were good enough to hold the truck in place, and there weren't any big trees near enough to do the job. There was a telephone pole nearby, and after thinking about it, I couldn't see any reason why it wouldn't work.

I hooked one end of the come-along cable to the rock and looped the other end securely around the telephone pole, where I situated myself with the come-along. I began rapidly moving the lever, *chicka, chicka, chicka,* and the slack began coming out of the line. I kept moving the lever, *chicka, chicka, chicka,* expecting to see the rock move. It wasn't moving yet, so I moved the lever as fast as I could, *chicka, chicka, chicka, chicka, chicka.*

I felt resistance, so I couldn't understand why the rock didn't seem to be moving. Suddenly I noticed a narrow shadow appear on the lawn in front of me. I looked up over my shoulder and got a big shock. The telephone pole was leaning over at a 45-degree angle. This wasn't good!

I quickly turned the come-along to reverse and worked the handle to release the tension: *chicka, chicka, chicka.* The tension came out of the cable, but the telephone pole remained at 45 degrees. Not only that, the telephone wires were strained to the max and looked like they'd break if the pole moved one more inch! I unhooked the cable from the pole and the rock and got the heck out of there.

By pure luck, no one had witnessed what had happened. The next day I sauntered into the weekly meeting of department heads.

Needless to say, the leaning telephone pole was the first topic of conversation. Everyone in the meeting, especially my boss, was totally stumped as to how something like this could have happened. I suggested that perhaps a large delivery truck had backed into it, but security said no big truck had been on campus that evening. I shook my head and looked just as mystified as the rest of them.

Nobody ever did figure out what had happened, and to this day, the case of the leaning telephone pole remains a mystery. I do know one thing though. I'm never hooking a come-along to a telephone pole again.

By the way, I waited until the new fiscal year, when I had sufficient funds to rent a backhoe, to move the rock. I'm happy to report that everything went well, and the rock looks great in its new home on the other end of campus.

PART 5

Gardening on the Home Front

Separate Beds

If your partner or spouse is a lazy bum and doesn't like to garden, you are among the luckiest people reading this book. You have the whole garden to yourself and are able to plant whatever you want. That's definitely not the case at my house.

I have the misfortune of being married to an expert gardener. Don't get me wrong. I wouldn't trade my wife, Mary, for anyone. The problem is that when we'd go out to garden, we'd barely make it 5 feet out the door before the arguments began. I'd say, "Let's plant a cimicifuga here," and she'd respond, "No way; this is the perfect spot for a ligularia!"

Whenever the neighbors saw us with hands and feet in the air at the same time, they'd say, "Uh-oh, it's garden wars again." We argued so often about what to plant, we finally realized that the only way to save our marriage was to have separate beds. No, not in the house, in the garden. We divided our yard into his and her beds.

Dividing the garden is the only way to go if both partners are avid gardeners. It made gardening more fun for both of us. I'm a rare-plant collector and I love searching out all kinds of treasures to plant in my side of the garden. It can get a bit competitive though. At one point, we made a rule that if one of us found a really cool, rare, and unusual plant, the other person couldn't plant one on their side of the garden for at least one year. It almost killed me when she went off to the nursery and came home with something really special that I was banned from planting on my side. Eventually we both began to cheat, so we canceled that rule. Nevertheless, we continue to seek out especially cool plants to make our side of the garden look better than the other side. When visitors come to see our garden, we stand shoulder to shoulder and demand, "Whose side do you like best?" I'm convinced that she's bribing all of those folks who keep voting for her side.

Of course, simply dividing the garden into his and her beds won't solve all of your domestic problems. A good example of what can go wrong happened when Mary and I visited one of our local nurseries together. Although we shopped separately, when we were ready to call it quits we regrouped in order to push our overflowing carts toward the cashier. That's when we both spotted a plant neither of us had ever seen before.

It was a eucomis, also known as a pineapple lily. Eucomis are summer-blooming bulbs with long strappy leaves and exotic white, pink, or violet flowers that resemble pineapples. We both had a variety of these South African lilies in our gardens, but this one was unlike any pineapple lily either of us had seen before. It was a new introduction called 'Oakhurst' featuring spectacular dark-red foliage. It was beautiful and rare—I knew I had to have it, and I suspected Mary was thinking the same thing. There was a serious problem, however. There was only one left.

We both acted like we hadn't seen it and kept pushing our carts along the pathway. Suddenly it turned into a Roller Derby match. We ran, elbowing and pushing, and almost knocked down a couple of elderly people who were in the way. Just as I thought I had it in my grasp, Mary dove and nabbed it right off the shelf. She wasn't at all humble about making the grab. She ran around holding the plant in the air like a football player who made the big catch for the touchdown. Shoppers were even clapping for her.

I was bummed, but I realized it wouldn't do any good to complain, so I accepted my fate. When we arrived home from the nursery, it was midafternoon and Mary said she was going to garden for a while before dinner. I, on the other hand, had to get ready right away to drive to Bellingham to give a garden talk that evening.

To my great dismay, when I started pulling the boxes out of the car, I noticed that the nursery employee had mixed up our plants in the boxes instead of keeping them separate as requested. There was no way I was going to let Mary decide which plants were which. We had a ten-minute garden war, until she finally promised that if I could prove that she swiped even one of my plants, she'd buy me a really good bottle of French wine. With that reassurance, I took off for Bellingham. I gave my talk, then went out to dinner with friends.

I didn't get back until near midnight, but as soon as I arrived home, I did what all good gardeners would do. I went out to the garage to see if Mary had swiped any of my plants. When I looked in the boxes, I was surprised beyond tweetle to see that she had somehow left the *Eucomis comosa* 'Oakhurst' in my box with the rest of my plants. I grabbed my digging spade and headed out to the garden. Even in the reflected moonlight, the pineapple lily made an exquisite pairing with the golden foliage of a *Caryopteris incana* 'Jason' Sunshine Blue.

Since I'd had a late night, I slept longer than usual the next morning. Mary had already finished breakfast and had headed out to garden when I sat down at the table. I watched her through the dining room window as she walked by the bed where I had planted the pineapple lily. She was pretty calm when she saw it. All she did was scream at the top of her lungs. When she came running in accusing me of stealing her plant, I said that since I'd found it in my box, I was sure she'd left it as a special gift to show me how much she loved me.

All I can say is that, if your partner is not a keen gardener, don't get him or her excited about it. Marriage counseling is getting so expensive!

Money Well Spent?

People often ask me what my wife, Mary, and I do with our dogs when we travel overseas together. We've always managed to find a dog sitter to stay in our house to take care of the pooches. Not only is it comforting to know that someone is in the house keeping an eye on things and giving the dogs loving care and attention, but the dogs are normally much better behaved when we arrive home.

If I am away during the dry summer months, I ask the house sitter to keep the plants watered, but I don't ask him or her to do any other garden chores. In all truth, I've almost never allowed anyone to weed or prune in my garden. It's filled with rare and unusual plants, and half the time even I'm hard pressed to tell if something coming up is a valued treasure or a weed.

Normally I avoid travel in spring and early summer because it is such a busy time in the garden. All the plants, especially weeds, are growing like mad, and even two or three weeks away can require a lot of work to catch up and make the garden presentable again. One year, however, we agreed to lead a tour to England in May, so that we could include the magnificent Chelsea Flower Show, an annual event in London. The problem was that I had already said yes to a tour of our home garden that would occur in early June, and a lot of skilled horticulturists would be on the tour. I knew that I would not have time to weed in the few days between returning home and the tour, so I made a major exception and asked our house sitter to keep the garden weeded while we were away. She was happy to do it, and I would pay her for weeding in addition to the daily fee for watching the pups.

Mary and I divide up the garden (see Separate Beds, page 133). Although I decided to hire the house sitter to weed my gardens, Mary said her gardens didn't need it because she thought she'd be able to squeeze in a day of weeding right before the tour. That was fine with me because if Mary didn't have enough time to straighten out her garden, the tour attendees would definitely prefer my side of the garden.

Before we left, I walked all of the gardens with the house sitter in order to go over watering schedules, but on my side I took extra time to show her exactly what to weed and which valued plants to watch out for. She agreed to err on the side of caution by only pulling what she was sure was a weed. I knew paying extra for all of that weeding was going to be expensive, but I left for the airport confident that my gardens would look great for the tour.

When we arrived home from our trip, I was amazed when I saw what an excellent weeding job our house sitter had done. I don't think she pulled out one valuable plant, and the gardens were weed-free and beautiful. There was only one little problem: she got mixed up and weeded only Mary's side of the garden!

I ended up killing myself trying to get my weedy mess looking half-decent by the day of the tour, while Mary happily spent her time moving plants, grooming, and trimming shrubs and perennials. On the big day, her garden had never looked more attractive. It seemed like everyone who came to the tour complimented her on how much better her side of the garden looked than mine. To this day, she loves to remind me that it was the best $20 an hour I've ever spent.

Living Ornaments on the Christmas Tree

Several years ago, while I was director of grounds at Seattle University, it was decided that a blue spruce tree had to come down to make room for building construction. The top of the tree was absolutely beautiful, and as it was just before Christmas, I decided to surprise my wife. I cut off the top to make a gorgeous 7-foot-tall Christmas tree and brought it home in a truck. Once I got the tree home, I had to work fast. The plan was to get it set up in the living room before Mary arrived home from work.

Everything went perfectly. I finished straightening it up in the stand just as Mary was getting home. The sky-blue color looked magnificent in our living room. That's when I noticed that our cat, Tiki, was staring at the ceiling, moving his head back and forth with that unmistakable look of a cat in pursuit of prey. When I followed his gaze, I was in for a bad surprise. A terribly bad surprise! Gazillions of red spiders were crawling all over the ceiling. There must have been a thousand of them. I knew that if Mary caught sight of the show on the ceiling, she was in for a way bigger surprise than I had planned.

I had to avert Mary's attention from the ceiling and the spiders, but Tiki was fixated on them, so I scooted him out the door just as Mary walked in. Then I got down on my knees like I was making a final adjustment, in order to keep her eyes aiming downward. Mary was totally surprised and loved the tree. I then announced that I had another surprise for her. I had made dinner reservations at our favorite restaurant, but we needed to leave quickly in order to be on time. Of course, I feigned great surprise when we arrived at the restaurant and they had no record of my reservation.

By the time we got home, the spiders were gone. I have no idea where they went, and I suspect I don't really want to know. I should add here that it was the sheer number of spiders that made me nervous about Mary's catching sight of them. Both Mary and I love spiders and allow spiders to live in our house. Spiders play a key role in helping to control harmful insects. As a group, they eat more harmful bugs than any other creature, hence the more spiders you can attract to your garden, or allow to live in your home, the less pest control you need to worry about. They also protect human health by eliminating disease-carrying insects such as flies and mosquitoes, and I'm convinced allowing spiders to live in our home is the reason why our pets rarely have flea problems.

But there's a limit to how many spiders you want to invite into your home. After the red spider experience, before I ever bring another treetop into the house, I'll thump the tweetle out of it by beating the base on concrete. Hopefully that would dislodge the majority of spiders or other little insects before they got the chance to hitchhike into the house. Still, I have to say that the blue spruce ended up looking great as our Christmas tree. At least it did until Tiki knocked off all of the ornaments, but that's a story for another time.

Water, Water Everywhere

Every garden should have at least one fountain. Water features add movement, reflection, and the sound of moving water to the garden, which is not only soothing to humans but attracts birds as well. It's not all that difficult to put a fountain in your garden. As long as you have access to electricity (hire an electrician to install an outdoor outlet), there is a wide variety of fountains available for purchase at local nurseries and garden statuary stores.

Then again, if you don't mind a bit of work, you can construct your own water feature. Making your own allows you to use your creativity to come up with something truly unique. I constructed all three of the water features in my garden, and I've never seen anything similar in any other garden.

I'll be the first to admit that constructing your own water feature can be a little challenging. The first one I put in is what I call the "waterfall," although it's really more of a burbling brook. Situated right next to the patio, the water begins at ground level and runs down a stream into a lower pond. The stream section is made up of preformed 2-foot-wide plastic liners that overlap, and the pond is a preformed plastic tub. The first task was to dig out the canyon for the stream to run down, as well as the hole at the bottom for the plastic tub.

It might have been better to plan this out before I began. I wasn't sure how deep to make the hole and I went overboard. By the time I stopped digging, the pond was so deep I could stand up straight in the hole and the top of my head was below ground level. I was thinking it might be pretty cool to have it that deep, but my wife, Mary, mentioned that if someone fell in, it would kill them and I realized I'd overdone it. I filled it back in to a safer depth. The preformed liners and pond never leak and are fairly indestructible. The only problem with using plastic parts is that they look fake. I hid the plastic by putting stones and driftwood over the liners and the rim of the tub. It worked well and now the waterfall looks and sounds like a mountain stream.

The second water feature came about when I bought a spectacular work of garden art. The piece was a beautifully colored 4-foot-diameter concrete sculpture of a *Tetrapanax papyrifer* 'Steroidal Giant' leaf, created by the famous garden artist duo David and George Lewis. Besides the gorgeous leaf, the artists supplied me with a 3-foot-tall concrete pillar and a large platform to support the leaf. The water is pumped to the top of the platform, where it bubbles up under the leaf to drip down into a water-filled pond. To make it all work, I had to construct the pond.

The first task was to dig a big hole. This time I knew not to overdo it and I made the hole 6 feet wide and 2 feet deep. Next I went to a nursery that specializes in water features to buy a rubber pond liner. A knowledgeable employee helped me calculate the liner size needed for the hole I had dug. He erred on the side of caution and cut the liner larger than necessary, so I could trim it down to the perfect size once I saw how it fit.

I did the job on a 76-degree F day, which was perfect because the warmth made the rubber liner soft and pliable. After trying the liner in the hole, I could see it was too big, so I laid it out flat on the lawn where I figured it would be easier to cut off the excess with a sharp pair of scissors. I was almost done making the cuts when I happened to step on the liner. I was working in bare feet and it felt like I was walking on hot coals: the liner was so hot it burned my feet!

That's when it hit me that the hot rubber might be cooking the grass underneath. I grabbed an edge of the liner and dragged it off the grass, but the damage was done. The grass was burnt to a crisp and dead as a doornail. For the rest of the summer, everyone who came to see my garden marveled at the perfect 6-foot-square patch of dead grass in the middle of my lawn and hardly noticed the fountain.

The fountain, however, turned out beautifully. I covered the liner with river rocks, which are colorful and rounded, lacking sharp edges that could poke holes in the liner. The leaf sculpture looked great for years, until a raccoon knocked it off and broke it to pieces. At first I was bummed, but now I have great fun placing lots of special garden art on the platform, including my favorite piece: a 2-foot-long bright-yellow glass banana slug specially commissioned from a local artist.

My third water creation featured another work of art by David and George Lewis. It's an old man's face they call *Bark Man*. It was originally fashioned from pieces of bark with a burl for his mouth, which became the mold for the concrete sculpture. *Bark Man*'s face is about 2 feet long and spits water down into a colorful basin 3 feet below. The only problem was that I didn't have anything on which to mount the old man's face. I needed to find something substantial enough to hold the heavy sculpture, yet natural enough to fit in with my garden filled with rare trees, shrubs, and perennials.

It didn't take me long to find something. A large weeping European birch tree (*Betula pendula*) had to be cut down to make room for construction on the Seattle University campus. It had attractive white bark, and I thought if I cut the top off, cut the side branches back, and planted it deep, it might be perfect. The question was how to get an extremely heavy 15-foot-long tree trunk into the back of my garden without destroying gazillions of valuable plants. Somehow I talked the SU garden staff into spending their valuable lunch hour helping me set it up in my garden.

It turned out to be a terribly difficult job, but we pulled it off without seriously damaging any of the surrounding plants. I wasn't so sure it looked that great, but after all of that work, I thought I could live with it.

I changed my mind when my wife came home from work and the first words out of her mouth were, "You aren't really going to leave that ugly thing in the garden, are you?" I didn't want to admit it, but she was right. It just didn't work. The trunk, with its stubbed-off branches and cutoff top, looked horrible.

Now I not only had to find something else, I had no idea how I was going to get rid of the ugly tree trunk.

I found the answer at the Northwest Flower and Garden show. One of the demonstration gardens featured huge stumps and snags to create an alpine look. I knew a snag would be perfect if I could find one. The garden creator was Dan Robinson, a well-known bonsai expert and owner of Elandan Gardens near Bremerton. He told me that he collected the stumps and snags from burn piles at the ocean to sell at his nursery. He said that once they had burned, they didn't tend to rot and would last practically forever. Days later I drove to his nursery and brought back an ancient-looking, indescribably heavy 12-foot-tall snag.

Then I talked my garden crew into coming back for another round of what I tried to describe as a fun-filled lunchtime activity in my garden (I ended up buying everyone lunch for a week). We somehow managed to heft that embarrassing birch trunk out and replace it with the snag. They even stood it up for me.

Interestingly, I discovered the whole crew had thought the birch looked horrendous when they brought it over. They just didn't mention it because they knew they'd have to haul the behemoth back out if they did!

The old man, as I call it, is by far my favorite fountain. The snag with the old man's face on it looks incredible, the sound of the water is perfect, and the birds absolutely love the fountain. The hummingbirds drink the water starting where it comes out of the old man's mouth and ride it down, drinking all the way to the basin. The other birds take turns sitting on the old man's lips, drinking and bathing as the water comes out of his mouth. All the birds take turns, that is, except the robins. Those piggy birds won't wait their turn and push the chickadees and nuthatches out of the way to get to the water. I have to admit, however, it's a lot of fun watching those silly robins try to squeeze their chubby bodies into the old man's 3-inch-wide lips in order to take a bath!

The good news is that you don't have to go to all of the work I did to put in a fountain. Nurseries and statuary stores sell highly attractive premade fountains that are easy to install and work great. They come in an amazing number of sizes and shapes, and price varies from under $50 to several thousand dollars.

There are a few things to consider before you put one in your landscape. First of all, put it in a key location where you can hear the water and watch the birds frolic. Place one near a patio or deck so that you can enjoy it when you hang out or eat dinner during the warmer months. Hummingbirds are attracted to moving water. I've yet to see a hummingbird visit the still water in a birdbath, but I often see them bathing in or drinking from fountains. Most any kind of fountain will attract hummingbirds as long as the water falls through open air such as the ones that consist of two or three bowls on different levels where the overflowing water cascades down from one tier to another. Of course, wherever you locate the fountain, you'll need to have an electric outlet in the vicinity.

Another consideration is making sure the fountain is out in the open. Never install a fountain under a tree or where leaves or needles will constantly fall into the water, or you'll be forced to skim and clean the water every day to keep it clean. Also, when installing your fountain, use a level to make sure it's perfectly even. A fountain that is askew just doesn't look right, and the water won't fall in an even pattern. Finally, don't make the mistake of putting in an overly loud water feature near where you spend your time relaxing in the garden. In my experience, the subtle sound of dripping water or a babbling brook is much more pleasant than a roaring waterfall.

Scoring a Petrified Stump at a Bargain Price

I'm a big fan of using stone as garden art. Stone adds a natural look and contrasts beautifully with most any plant, especially ones with fine foliage. One of my favorite types of stone is petrified wood. I think it's beautiful and enhances the garden, especially in a natural setting or in a rock garden.

You used to be able to go over to the Vantage area of Eastern Washington and simply take pieces of petrified wood, but now there are strict rules against that practice. These days petrified wood is hard to come by, and if you find it for sale at a rock center, it's expensive.

That's why I became excited when a friend told me that an acquaintance in his rock club was selling his collection of petrified wood. I figured, with my bargaining skills, I might be able to score some cool pieces at a good price. My friend and I set out on our mission.

Unfortunately for me, the man selling the petrified wood knew the value of his stone and was asking incredibly high prices. I bought only a couple of small pieces to use in one of my water features. Then, when we were leaving, something special caught my eye. It was a petrified stump buried about a third deep near a pond in his garden. The stone was white with an amber tinge; better yet, it had a sunken bowl in the middle, making it perfect to use as a birdbath. I figured if I could get him to sell it, I'd fork out at least $1,500.

When I asked him how much he'd be willing to sell it for, he amazed me by replying, "Fifty bucks." When I asked him if I heard him right, he said, "Yup, fifty bucks, but you've got to take it right now."

The stump looked like it weighed between 300 and 400 pounds, but I knew I had to have it. He loaned us some shovels and we dug it out. Then we rolled it over to my fairly new Toyota hatchback. My friend wasn't a whole lot bigger than I am, and there was no way we were going to be able to lift it into the car.

With a great deal of effort, we somehow managed to roll it into the back of my Toyota. It took an equal effort to haul it back out of the car when we arrived at my house. The petrified stump is now planted a third deep in my rock garden, and it looks fantastic surrounded by a wide variety of spectacular plants. It's definitely one of the most attractive pieces of art in my garden and a favorite bathing spot for the birds in my front yard. OK, I admit it cost a couple of thousand to repair my car, but hey, I got the petrified stump for fifty bucks!

Oops: Be Careful When Placing Stone

As spectacular as petrified wood looks in a garden setting, nothing can match the feel and beauty that outcropping stones bring to a garden. Heavy, rough large stones are sculptures of nature. Set firmly in the ground, outcropping stones create a feeling of strength, stability, and constancy. Surrounding them with plantings suggest growth and activity, seasonal change, and the cycles of life. Contrast of this kind is what the Japanese refer to as the "union of opposites" and it's an effect that only the use of stone can achieve.

Most of us are used to seeing outcropping stone in Japanese gardens or alpine settings, but I'm an advocate for using them in most any kind of setting. At Seattle University, I used them in mixed borders and English-style perennial beds, as well as in woodland and native gardens. Besides creating beauty, adding large outcropping stones makes it easier to design an attractive garden. That's because groupings of large stone add structure, supplying a framework for your plantings.

Of course, you can't simply buy some big stones, stick them in the ground, and expect them to look natural. If you decide you want to incorporate stone, the first step is to visit gardens with beautiful rock work to note how skilled designers enhance the landscape with stone. There are all sorts of gardens with great stonework. Often you'll find gardens with great outcropping formations by simply going for a walk in your neighborhood, but it also pays to visit public gardens where rocks play a key role. Famous Japanese and rock gardens are a good place to start, but don't overlook university and hospital campuses as well.

Since all settings are different, note the different colors, sizes, and shapes of the rocks that were used while considering how they would look in your garden. Pay special attention to the size of the rocks. In my experience, big rocks almost always look good even in small gardens, but stones that are too small, especially in a big garden, can look out of proportion, contrived, and artificial.

Finally, while you're checking out the stone landscapes, observe how the designer grouped the rocks to create a natural look. You'll notice the most natural-looking formations are made up of rugged stones grouped in odd numbers. Stones grouped in even numbers create a feeling of orderliness and completion that is never found in nature and feels artificial.

Next, visit a stone yard. Depending on where you live and how big the stone yard is, you're likely to be amazed at all of the different types of rocks on display. You'll see a wide variety of granite and basalt, huge stone columns, limestone, river boulders, lava rocks, and much more. It can be quite difficult to decide on the type of stone you want to use. Generally, sticking to one type of rock works best.

Once you've decided on the type of stone you're going to use, the real fun begins. Walk through the yard to choose each individual stone, which will be marked for later delivery. Here are a few helpful tips: Avoid the inexpensive stone that was recently dug from underground quarries. Newly dug stone usually has a shiny, bright appearance that looks out of place in the landscape. It's worth spending a bit more to purchase weathered stone, which is much more attractive and natural looking.

At the same time, avoid going with weathered rock that has moss growing on it. You pay a lot for the moss, and it usually dies out once the stone is placed in its new climatic conditions in your garden. Moss does add a natural look, but don't worry about it. Outcropping stones seem to attract moss and lichen, and in many climates, especially in the Pacific Northwest, the stones will be moss covered in record time.

Once you've picked out the individual rocks, the next decision is how to actually put them in your garden. There are three ways you can do this. First, you could hire a landscape company that specializes in rock work. This is the most expensive route, but if you do your homework and find a talented designer, chances are you'll end up with something attractive and natural looking. This is probably the best option if the stones are to be placed near existing trees or plantings or will be located in areas of the garden that are hard to access.

If the location is accessible by truck, you can go with the second option, which is to have the stone yard place them for you. The stone yard will have big flatbed trucks with huge arms equipped with a platypus-shaped device on the end, specially designed for picking up and moving rocks. All you have to do is dig the hole. They'll bring the rocks on the truck and use the platypus-equipped arm to place the stones where you want them. I've used this service several times, and most of the folks who bring the rock are talented rock setters. They'll work with you to set them up and angle them just the way you want them.

The third option is by far the most fun and probably the least expensive method. You can rent a backhoe and place the stone yourself. If you've never run one, I suggest spending a half day of practice digging and placing stone in a back area of your garden. Make sure you call to have utilities checked before you dig in any area of the garden. Running a backhoe is great fun.

I occasionally operated one to place stone in Seattle University landscapes that I designed and installed. I wasn't the most talented person on the staff when it came to running backhoes, but I was reasonably proficient.

At this point I probably should mention that, unless you're quite familiar with heavy equipment, it's probably not a good idea to use the backhoe method if the rocks are going to be placed near a house or other structure. Having said that, I rented a backhoe and used it to place a huge rock quite near my house. My confidence was based on the fact that I had already placed several large groupings of stone in my front garden using a backhoe when we moved in a few years earlier. This time, the rock I was going to place was big. It weighed about 2 tons and had been given to me by the university after it was dug up to make room for new building construction. It was a magnificent granite column, and I was planning to stand it up right next to the house immediately after we had completed a major remodel.

At first the project seemed to get off to a good start. The utility check found no utilities to worry about, my new stone sat ready in my driveway, and the backhoe was delivered right on time.

There was one little problem, however. The rental yard somehow got mixed up and delivered the wrong backhoe. The only backhoe I'd ever operated, and the one I ordered from the rental yard, was a CASE backhoe. The one they delivered was a John Deere. The controls were the exact opposite.

Anyone with a brain would have called the rental yard to have them exchange the John Deere for the CASE. But being the great equipment operator that I am, I was totally confident that I could make the adjustment.

I didn't just put the rock through the side of the house—I followed it with the bulldozer!

You know the terrifying feeling you get when you realize you've just run into a hornet's nest? That's the feeling I had when I saw the look on my wife's face when she came out the back door. I thought, *Should I run or stand my ground and take it like a man?* I ran! When she caught me, I explained that I had no choice but to use the machine to pull the rock out of the side of the house. She wisely decided the best course of action was to leave and let me do it without having to watch, so she called a friend and went out for a drink . . . or two.

I managed to use the machine to pull the rock out of the side of the house, but a huge gaping hole remained, and all of the neighbors came by to compliment my skill as a backhoe operator.

I'm happy to report that, when I called our insurance agent and asked if they paid for little "boo-boos," she said they would pay to have the damage repaired, but only once.

Needless to say, I've been banned from bringing backhoes home and have had to attend Backhoes Anonymous ever since. Considering how expensive marriage counseling has become, if you're thinking about placing some big outcropping stones in your garden, going the platypus route or hiring a crew might just be the way to go!

PART 6

Plant Potpourri

Brussels Sprouts: Love 'Em or Hate 'Em

I'm famous for championing brussels sprouts. I really do love them, and I eat them practically every day. Perhaps I'm spouting off too much about how much I like them. Sometimes people bring me special treats when they attend one of my garden talks, and I have to admit it's a bit of a letdown when I look into a bag of goodies to find they've brought me brussels sprouts rather than chocolate chip cookies!

I talk about them so much because I find it hilarious that, in almost every couple, one person loves brussels sprouts while the other detests them. I suspect many boomers are turned off by memories of growing up with moms like mine, who believed you had to boil them until they screamed for mercy to make sure they were safe to eat. Overboiling brussels sprouts brings out the stinky odor of glucosinolate sinigrin, an organic compound that contains sulfur.

I think that's one of the reasons my wife, Mary, hates them. She calls them my little boogers and runs out of the house if I accidentally overcook them. If your partner or spouse abhors them, just to keep life interesting, sneak a few of the little delights into whatever your partner is cooking for dinner when he or she leaves the room. It's so fun to see the look on his or her face when one of the little depth charges emerges during dinner!

Brussels sprouts have only recently gained popularity. They used to be so reviled, a 2008 survey conducted by Heinz found brussels sprouts were the most hated of all vegetables in the USA. That's why I'm so amazed that, over the last few years, brussels sprouts have made such a fantastic comeback in the culinary world. I'd like to take credit for it, but I suspect their return to epicurean grace may be due to recognition of their health benefits. Brussels sprouts are a great source of protein, iron, and potassium, and are loaded with vitamin C, fiber, and folate.

Interestingly, the same organic compound, glucosinolate sinigrin, that makes them smell bad when you overcook them is also crammed with powerful cancer-fighting components. If you don't overcook them, brussels sprouts won't give off the slightest bad odor and are quite delicious.

Don't feel bad if you've had a hard time growing brussels sprouts in your home garden. They're actually quite difficult to grow. In the Puget Sound region, brussels sprouts are grown in the Skagit Valley, where they get plenty of sunshine but summer temperatures tend to stay relatively cool. Brussels sprouts don't like hot, sunny conditions; hence it's best to start the seeds indoors (or buy starts at your local nursery) sufficiently early to be transplanted into the garden in early April. Plant the starts 24 inches apart and work in ½ cup of organic tomato food under each plant. Avoid using fertilizer that is high in nitrogen because that encourages foliage at the expense of sprout formation.

The most common problem with growing brussels sprouts is that the sprouts don't size up before winter sets in. There are a number of factors that can keep that from happening. The first consideration is variety. Brussels sprouts that take a long time to mature sometimes don't form sprouts until it's too late in the season to size up well. Varieties that ripen early, such as *Brassica oleracea gemmifera* 'Franklin', usually form nice large sprouts before frost occurs.

The worst thing you can do to brussels sprouts is to allow starts to become root-bound in their containers before planting them out. That stresses the plants, causing them to bolt by going to seed and could result in no sprout production at all. Finally, even if you do everything right, unseasonable temperatures (too hot or too cold) may prevent sprouts from forming. Make sure the soil stays evenly moist, especially in hot weather.

When it comes to growing brussels sprouts, the most irritating problem is when huge populations of aphids find their way into the sprouts. Prevent this by washing the aphids off the plants with a daily blast of water from the hose nozzle during the period when sprouts are forming. If the aphids do get into the sprouts, you can get most of them out by soaking the sprouts in salted water before you cook them. Take it from one who knows: Don't let your sprout-challenged spouse see you do this. I guarantee that if she sees all the aphids floating in the water, she will not become a convert!

If possible, wait to harvest until temperatures turn cold. The sprouts can easily withstand light frosts, and freezing weather triggers physiological changes that make them taste sweet as sugar. Harvest the ripe ones at the bottom, snapping them off and removing the leaves in your way as you work on up the stalk. The sprouts higher up the stalk will continue to mature until you pick them. If your sprouts aren't sizing up by mid-September, pinch out the growing point at the top of the stem. As long as the lower sprouts are close to ½ inch in diameter, most of the sprouts will increase to full size within about two weeks.

I prepare brussels sprouts in a lot of ways and even put them in quesadillas! One of my favorite cooking methods is to simply cut the sprouts in half, drizzle with olive oil, sprinkle with garlic, pepper, and salt, then roast them.

I must admit, however, that no one can make brussels sprouts taste better than Chef Lynne Vea at Puget Consumers Co-op (PCC). I had the great fortune of shooting cooking segments with her on my *Gardening with Ciscoe* TV show. We cooked all kinds of wonderful dishes together, and I have to say, that woman can make anything taste good, even beets! On the days when we filmed the cooking segments, Mary would be waiting at the door in eager anticipation to see what gourmet delights I'd come home with.

One day, Lynne showed how to make pan-seared brussels sprouts with apples, bacon, shallots, and rosemary (search for the recipe at PCCMarkets.com). Mary was glum when she saw what I brought home that day, but that was fine with me, as I would have it all to myself. I had to head out to perform my live Friday-night TV show and would be home late to eat dinner.

I must have raved about that recipe a little too much because, soon after I left for the studio, Mary gave in and tried a bite. Evidently she liked it. When I returned home it was all gone! There is truth in the old saying "Everything is better with bacon."

Finally, a couple of warnings regarding brussels sprouts. If you ever decide to surprise those little trick-or-treaters by offering them brussels sprouts as a treat on Halloween, make sure you have a backup bowl of candy to give out, just in case. I didn't, and I found brussels sprouts in some very surprising places the following morning.

Also be careful if you give brussels sprouts nicknames. Meeghan and I were shooting our TV show at Swansons Nursery when I discovered brussels sprouts starts on one of the shelves. Without thinking, and on camera, I exclaimed, "Look, Meeghan, they have love nibbles!" After everyone regained their composure, my producer wanted to make sure she understood exactly what I'd said.

Later, while watching that show on the following Saturday, I couldn't help but break into laughter when that part of the show was accompanied with a caption that read "He said 'nibbles.'" So feel free to call brussels sprouts love nibbles—just make sure to pronounce the *b*'s carefully!

Grow Spuds in a Container

Growing potatoes in a container is a lot of fun. It's more for amusement than production, but sometimes you end up with a pretty good harvest. One thing's for sure: kids love taking part in the experiment, and it's a great way to get them excited about gardening.

Any clean 15-gallon or bigger plastic garbage can or similar container will do. Don't use galvanized steel cans because they rust out. Begin by drilling several ½-inch-wide drainage holes in the bottom and up the sides about 2 inches from the bottom. Good drainage is essential. If the roots sit in constantly wet soil, the plants will rot.

Next, fill the can 6 inches deep with houseplant potting soil. Use potting soil that contains slow-release fertilizer, or feed with a balanced (equal numbers) organic soluble houseplant fertilizer every two weeks until the vines show signs of dying back in late summer. Buy starter potatoes online or at your local nursery and plant them whole, 5 inches apart, just under the soil surface. Plant only one variety of potato in each can.

Water the potatoes in, and before long growth will occur. As soon as the vines grow to 4 inches tall, cover all but the top inch of the lowest-growing vine with potting soil. As the vines continue to grow, keep covering all but the top inch every time they put on another 4 inches. Potatoes form only along vines that are covered regularly, so allowing excessive uncovered growth to occur usually results in a reduced harvest.

Eventually the vines will grow out of the top of the container, which by now will be full of soil, and the vines will begin to bloom. By this time, spuds that formed along the covered vines should be sizing up, and you can reach in and pick the biggest ones you can find. These are new potatoes. They don't store but are delicious steamed, especially if you follow Julia Child's advice that everything tastes better with extra butter!

As summer progresses, continue to water and fertilize regularly while harvesting a few new potatoes from time to time. In late summer or fall, depending on the variety you're growing, the vines will begin to wither. Once they've died back completely, cut the vines right back to the top of the soil in the container and wait a week before harvesting. That will give the skins time to harden enough to store well.

Now comes the fun part. Both adults and kids can't wait to check out the bounty when you dump out the can. You never know what you'll find. One year there were only six potatoes. The smallest was the size of my little fingernail, while the biggest was the size of a Volkswagen Beetle. Another year, I was delighted to discover thirty-five good-size 'German Butterball' potatoes, while my all-time record harvest was fifty-five softball-size purple-skinned 'Peruvian Blues'.

I always used a clean garbage can for this project—that is, until I gave a garden talk at a conference in Juneau, Alaska, in the early 1990s. Jim Hole, owner of Hole's Greenhouses in Edmonton, Alberta, also gave a talk at the conference. In his slide show, he had a picture of a special container that he sells at his nursery. Made in England especially for growing potatoes, these containers offer some big advantages over growing spuds in a garbage can. The plastic sides reflect heat, preventing it from getting too hot inside the container, which can be a problem with darker-colored garbage cans. It also comes predrilled with holes and contains a ridge to elevate the bottom to enhance drainage. And because of the way potatoes grow, with the deeper ones being larger, these English containers have a special door near the bottom that enables you to reach in to the lower section of the container to harvest the larger new potatoes, an almost impossible feat when reaching in from the top of a tall garbage can.

When I returned home, I tried to find somewhere local to buy one of these English containers, but after calling around I was disappointed to learn that none of my local nurseries carried anything similar. This was during the time my TV cohost, Meeghan Black, and I were filming garden tips that were shown regularly on KING 5 news shows, and I was always looking for ideas. In early April, I thought it would be fun to show viewers how to plant spuds in a container. Although I could have used a garbage can, I wanted to try out a fancy English container and was determined to buy one.

Looking back, I don't know what I was thinking. The shoot was scheduled for early the next week and I had only three days to come up with one of those special containers. I called Jim Hole in Edmonton. He was willing to send me one, but the problem was that to arrive in time, he would need to ship it express.

The container came on time and cost only $20. The shipping, on the other hand, ended up costing me about $100!

On TV filming day, we used the English potato-growing container to show viewers how to grow spuds in a container. I chose to plant 'Peruvian Blue' potatoes because I'd had great success with growing them in containers in the past. I promised viewers that we would show the harvest on TV at the end of the season.

Evidently the segment was quite popular. As part of the tip, we gave out the phone number of Hole's Greenhouses in case some viewers wanted to order containers from Canada. A couple of days after the segment aired on TV, I received a phone call from Jim Hole. He told me that he had ordered about a hundred of those containers from an English supplier years ago, but they had been sitting in a storage room unsold. After the piece showed on KING 5, he sold out in two days!

Harvest time came and, as promised, we showed the big potato harvest on TV. Meeghan and I dumped out the contents of the container and there were about 200 potatoes, but to my chagrin, and Meeghan's uncontrollable laughter, the biggest one was the size of a Ping-Pong ball! There was even one red potato in there. I suspect Meeghan stuck it in there as a joke, but to this day, she's never confessed.

Embarrassing as it was to show that particular harvest on TV, I'm happy to report it was a onetime failure. The following year, my English container yielded thirty decent-size spuds, and subsequent harvests have been mostly successful. Fortunately, people I've met who ordered a container after watching the segment usually tell me they've generally had decent harvests as well. The other good news is that you can now find specially made inexpensive potato-growing containers at local nurseries and online. They may not be as cool as my English one, but from everything I've heard, they work just as well and won't cost you $100 shipping!

Don't Count Your Giant Pumpkins Before They're Harvested

One year, just for the fun of it, I challenged the gardeners at Seattle University to a giant pumpkin–growing contest. The prize for the biggest pumpkin was a stash of extra-large peanut butter chocolate chip cookies, one to the winner from each contestant. I knew the competition was going to be tough, but being that I was the head gardener, I was determined to win.

It's not the easiest thing to grow a giant pumpkin, but if you have enough garden space and like growing odd plants, it's an interesting challenge. Kids love to help in this project, but since all of my "kids" have four feet, they didn't get overly excited about it.

If you want to grow a really big pumpkin, the first thing to do is set aside a large sunny space in your vegetable garden. The champion pumpkin growers say that growing a single big one can cover about 1,200 square feet, approximately a 40-foot-diameter circle. They are, however, growing thousand-pounders. You won't need that much room, but to be safe don't plant other plants anywhere nearby. Giant pumpkins don't appreciate competition. Before you plant, make sure the soil is well amended with compost, and test the soil in the fall to find out if any nutrients are lacking. If the soil is somewhat acid, add lime as necessary to maintain a pH close to neutral.

To grow a really big pumpkin, you need to start with special seed for giant pumpkins. The competitive growers pay big bucks for seed from past champion pumpkins, but home growers can find reasonably priced quality giant pumpkin seed online from local mail-order nurseries such as Territorial Seed and Nichols Garden Nursery.

Germinate the seeds indoors in early May. Air temperatures should be between 65 and 75 degrees F, with soil temperatures between 70 and 90 degrees F. Plant the starts in the garden in late May, after the last frost, and work ½ cup of 5-10-10 organic fertilizer into the soil around the starts. About two weeks before planting, warm the garden soil by laying down black plastic. You're ready to plant when the soil temperature remains at about 60 degrees F. If you're really into it, buy or construct a hoop house to create warmer conditions early in the season.

Like all squash plants, pumpkins are monoecious, meaning they bear separate male and female flowers on the same plant. Normally bees carry pollen from the male flowers to the females, but with declining bee populations, the flowers may not receive adequate pollination. If that happens, the fruit will rot and wither away soon after it forms, greatly delaying your start for a big pumpkin.

Give Mama Nature a hand by using male flowers to pollinate five female flowers each. It's easy to tell the flowers apart. The female flower has what looks like a little squash under it, while male flowers have long, thin stems. Make sure that plenty of the pollen from the male flower ends up on the end of the pistil, the part sticking out of the middle of the female flower.

Once the fruit grow to over 6 inches in diameter, remove all but the biggest pumpkin. If you're worried the pumpkin might fail, keep the two biggest, but once the biggest one is healthy and strong, remove the smaller one. It's important that all of the plant's energy goes to only one pumpkin. Place a large piece of Styrofoam or a wooden pallet under the pumpkin before it gets too heavy. That will keep the pumpkin's bottom from rotting and will make it easier to lift and transport later. Cover the pumpkin with shade cloth once it reaches 24 to 36 inches in diameter. That will help keep the pumpkin's skin from hardening and cracking in the hot mid- to late-summer sun.

Bury vines at the leaf nodes whenever you notice roots beginning to grow out of the vine, but don't bury the leaves. The roots that form at the buried nodes will suck up moisture and help prevent wind from rolling the vines. Feed with organic 20-20-20 fertilizer every two weeks. Water regularly to keep the soil moist, but avoid wetting the leaves as that could lead to disease. Once the main vine has reached about 16 feet long, pinch off the end and the tips of the side shoots to divert energy from vine growth to the fruit. As the season progresses, continue to cut off any flowers that form on the vines.

When it gets late in the season, be aware that it takes only a couple of weeks of nighttime temperatures under 50 degrees F to harm pumpkins, causing them to rot. Usually the best time to harvest is as soon as the skin turns bright orange. Once you pick your pumpkin, the color will stop developing, so if it isn't coloring up, or if you want to leave it in the ground longer to let it grow bigger, you'll need to protect both the pumpkin and the foliage from cold temperatures. On cool evenings, cover your pumpkin with a heavy quilt, while using row-crop cover to protect the foliage. Make sure to remove the coverings every morning.

I named my giant pumpkin Gertrude, and I'm proud to say that she grew to be a real honker. Although I never weighed her, she looked like she was almost 200 pounds. I was sure I was going to win, and as harvest day neared, I annoyed the living tweetle out of my fellow workers with my incessant bragging about my monstrous pumpkin.

One important tip: if you are in a pumpkin-growing contest, I strongly suggest you guard it in your bedroom the night before the weigh-in! Imagine my surprise when I sauntered out to harvest my prize pumpkin on the morning of the contest, only to find that Gertrude was missing and had been replaced by a can of pumpkin pie filling!

Eventually my cohorts gave my pumpkin back, and I claimed my bragging rights (and the cookies) as the champion pumpkin grower on the SU grounds crew. As proud as I was, I can't even imagine the esteem you would feel if your pumpkin was crowned the winner at one of the world giant pumpkin championships.

If you haven't ever attended one of these events, you haven't lived until you see one of these humongous champions up close. These sagging monsters are nothing like the round pumpkins we carve into jack-o'-lanterns. The weight gives them bizarre shapes, and the really big ones have midridge bulges that make sumo wrestlers look like ballerina dancers. There's a big cash prize for the biggest pumpkin, but just like me, giant pumpkin growers aren't in it for the money. It's all about the prestige you feel for growing the biggest pumpkin. Although I have to admit, those cookies sure tasted good!

Life of a Garden Writer

Upright sedums are wonderful additions to the garden. Low maintenance with bold succulent foliage and showy late-season flowers, they're the perfect plant to liven up the fall garden. Bees love the bunches of pink blossoms, and birds feast on the showy seed heads after they fade in early winter.

'Autumn Joy' has been a longtime favorite, but now there are sedums with spectacular foliage to go along with their beautiful blooms, rendering them a must for the perennial garden. If you like variegated foliage, you'll love 'Autumn Charm'. It glows all season long with gray-green leaves edged in butter yellow. In August it's completely covered with light-pink flowers that turn a russet red in October.

Another eye-catcher is 'Maestro'. This one forms a sturdy clump of blue-green foliage that gradually turns purple. The huge flower heads, which can reach 7 inches across, open to rich pink. If you are into dark foliage, it's hard to beat 'Postman's Pride'. It was discovered by a Belgian postal carrier who found it growing in his garden. Its deep blue-purple foliage more than makes up for its sprawling growth habit, especially when its purple buds open to reveal pinkish-red flowers that turn burgundy in fall.

The champ, however, when it comes to dark foliage has to be 'Black Jack'. Not only does it boast a strong upright habit, the foliage is the deepest purple of any upright sedum. The spring growth emerges deceivingly light purple, but by early summer it turns so dark, you'll think it's black. In fall, brilliant pink flower heads can measure a whopping 8 inches across!

Upright sedums are drought tolerant. They are easy to grow and pest-free as long as they are in a sunny location with decent drainage. They do have one weakness, however. If you grow them in your mixed border in rich, moisture-holding soil, the normally upright stems tend to get too heavy and flop over. Once this happens, you practically have to hog-tie them to a stake to keep them upright, and no matter how you do it, they look horrible.

After trying various methods to prevent the flopping problem on my upright sedums, I discovered that the best solution for plants that are beginning to flop is to cut them down two-thirds of the way to the ground in the first week of June. When you do this, you'll be convinced that you just murdered your plant. Don't panic: your sedum will grow back at a record pace but it won't end up as tall. Instead it will form a dense dome that, in fall, will be a blaze of color covered with multitudes of smaller, but just as showy, flowers.

After a couple of years of experimenting with cutting sedums back, I was sure that my technique worked, so I wrote it up in a *Seattle Post-Intelligencer* article to come out the first week of June. After the article appeared in the morning edition, I was walking my pup Kokie later that same day when we heard what sounded like a car going into an uncontrollable skid right behind us. We both spun around, expecting to see a horrible accident. Instead, we saw an elderly woman rolling down her window as she came to an abrupt stop in the middle of the road.

"Are you Ciscoe?" she gruffly asked.

When I answered in the affirmative, she said, "Are you sure you're right about cutting sedums down like that?"

I said yes and she shouted, "You better be!" Then she rolled up the window as she screeched away down the road.

Her plant must not have died, because I never saw her again.

Make Your Paperwhites Tipsy

Paperwhites are popular bulbs to force over the holidays. The fragrance is divine, and it's a fun, easy project to do with kids. Start with a watertight vase. It can be practically any size, but deeper ones seem to work best. Fill the container with decorative stones or colored marbles, making sure to leave about 4 inches of space on top for the bulbs. Then nestle in as many bulbs as will fit, pointed side up, on top of the marbles or stones. Squeeze them in tight. Paperwhites look best in large groupings, and the cozy fit of the bulbs will help keep the stems from falling over.

Finish the composition by covering all but the top quarter of the bulbs with the same decorative material as you used to fill the vase. It's now time to fill the container with water. Fill only until the water touches the base of the bulbs. Keeping the base in contact with water will stimulate growth, but be careful not to add too much. If the bulbs sit in water, they'll rot. Keep the container in a cool room (around 65 degrees F if possible), refilling as needed to make sure the water reaches the base of the bulbs at all times.

Keep an eye on your paperwhites, and when growth begins, move the container to a sunny window. Keep it there while giving the vase a quarter turn each day until the flowers open. Then locate the container where you can display it, in an area out of direct sunshine in order to make the flowers last longer.

The biggest problem with paperwhites is that they grow so fast in our warm homes, the stems get too tall to support the weight of the flower and fall over. Once that happens, all you can do is try to stake them or tie the stems together. Suddenly what was supposed to be a pleasing decorative display loses its appeal.

Fortunately, there's a simple trick that can prevent your paperwhites from toppling over, but you have to do it before they flower. When the stems have reached about 5 inches tall, add vodka to the water. Much as you might expect this treatment to make the plants tipsy, it actually burns the roots and slows the growth. The stems will grow to only about half of their normal height, but the flowers will be just as large and fragrant as ever. You do have to use care not to get the plants too drunk in this process. As a general guideline, aim for one part vodka to about seven parts water.

If you give them too much booze for the amount of water, your inebriated paperwhites might not only embarrass you by acting drunk in front of visitors, they're also likely to have so much fun partying they'll never bloom.

In case you're wondering about planting them outdoors, paperwhites are native to warm climates around the Mediterranean. In Zone 8 or above, where freezing weather is relatively rare, plant your paperwhites outdoors as soon as they're finished blooming, and with luck you'll have wonderfully fragrant paperwhites flowering in your garden every spring for years to come. In climates where freezing winter weather is common, toss the bulbs in the compost bin because, even fortified with vodka, they aren't hardy enough to survive the winter outdoors.

I Humbly Admit That I'm the Champ

I'm not exactly sure when I planted my variegated azara (*Azara microphylla* 'Variegata'), but it was probably in the early 1990s. Variegated azaras are highly attractive trees with tiny creamy white-and-green variegated evergreen leaves. These trees typically reach 15 to 25 feet in height with a spread of about 10 feet. They have a graceful form with arching branches. In late winter clusters of intensely fragrant tiny flowers appear that smell like a mix of chocolate and vanilla, followed by orange-red berries that last well into fall.

The variegated azara originated from a mutation that someone discovered on an *Azara microphylla*, a small tree with tiny glistening green leaves native to Chile and Argentina. Many attractive and unusual trees and shrubs are the result of a mutation. If you have a beautiful red-leaved Japanese maple in your garden, it most likely came from a mutation that occurred on a green-leaved Japanese maple variety.

Mutations are often discovered when a nursery owner or a home gardener notices unusual growth coming from a branch on a tree or shrub. It could take the form of a shoot with contorted growth or, as in the case of my azara, a branch with variegated leaves. Cuttings of the unusual branch are rooted, and voilà: a new plant, never before seen on earth, is created and eventually becomes available to the nursery trade.

I bought my variegated azara when I stopped by Christianson's Nursery in Mount Vernon on my way home from giving a garden talk on Orcas Island. I'd never seen a variegated azara before. The seedling came in a 4-inch pot and was only about 3 inches tall. There was minimal information on the tag but it stated the tree was hardy to Zone 8 and could take sun or light shade. I had no idea if it would survive in my garden.

Soon after I planted it, the tree took off and grew at a rapid pace. About ten years later, Dan Hinkley, cofounder of the famous Heronswood Garden, came to visit my garden.

It turned out that Dan had sold those exact variegated azara starts to Christianson's Nursery, and he was amazed by how tall my tree had grown. For a number of years after Dan's visit, I didn't pay much attention to how fast it continued to grow until Arthur Lee Jacobson stopped by for a visit in 2017. Arthur is a tree expert who has written eight books, including *Trees of Seattle*.

In that book, he describes a number of champion trees that are the tallest of their species in Washington State. It just so happened that he had been out searching for champion trees that day. While we were talking, my wife, Mary, asked Arthur if he'd ever seen my variegated azara. Arthur practically fell over when he saw the tree. To my great surprise he told me that without a doubt, my 30-foot-plus variegated azara was the champion tree of its kind in Washington State.

There was only one problem: my variegated azara had reverted. Trees or shrubs that originate from mutations sometimes revert and produce branches of the original tree or shrub they came from. If this happens, it's important to remove any reverted branches as soon as they are noticed. Those green leaves contain higher levels of energy-producing chlorophyll than colored or variegated ones and the stronger growth can take over, leaving you with a green tree instead of the colorful one you brought home from the nursery.

The reversion that occurred in my azara was way up at the top of the tree, and the green-leaved branch grew upward at a faster rate than the surrounding branches. It gave the tree an unattractive top-heavy two-tone look.

I knew the reversion was there but didn't really want to climb to the top of my azara to remove it. Fortunately, Arthur is a talented tree climber and a professional pruner to boot. He agreed to tackle the job for a reasonable fee, and even after the reversion was removed, Arthur was certain that my tree was still by far the tallest variegated azara in the state.

Not long after he pruned the tree, I received a surprising e-mail from Arthur. He had been checking with colleagues from around the country, and it turned out that my variegated azara was the tallest one in the United States. Then a couple of weeks later, the real shock came. After checking with tree experts from quite a number of different countries, Arthur informed me that my variegated azara was the tallest one in the world!

I can't tell you how excited I was to learn that I had the tallest tree of its kind on earth in my garden. Ever since I found out, I haven't been able to stop bragging about it. OK, I admit I might be overdoing it a bit. I've noticed that a few of my friends roll their eyes when I remind them about it for the tenth or eleventh time. Hey, how can I have the tallest tree of its kind on the planet growing in my garden without bragging about it?

Plant a Real Stinker

It always creates quite a stir when a corpse flower (*Amorphophallus titanum*) blooms in a local greenhouse. Seeing one of these rare honkers in flower is an unforgettable experience. Native to rain forests in Sumatra and Java, these big mamas produce some of the largest flowers on earth, with colorful blossoms that can reach more than 10 feet tall. Underground they produce a corm, a modified root similar to a bulb, that can weigh more than 300 pounds.

Amorphophallus are members of the aroid family, and are commonly referred to as arums. They're relatives of calla lilies, and like all of the plants in that family, the flower consists of a vase-shaped structure known as a *spathe* made up of modified leaves or bracts that surround a central upright flower spike, the *spadix*.

The spathe on the corpse flower is striped green and white on the outside and is a deep meaty red within. The yellowish-brown spadix can reach almost 6 feet tall and contains both male and female flowers.

This beautiful combination is a fascinating sight, but the attribute that grabs everyone's attention—and has them running for the door—is the overpowering stench of rotting flesh. This giant plant evolved to attract carrion beetles and flesh flies for pollination purposes. These insects feed on dead animals or lay their eggs in rotting meat. The flowers open in the late afternoon, and the odor gradually increases from late evening into the middle of the night, when carrion beetles and flesh flies are the most active;

then the stench tapers off toward morning. The spadix even heats up, thereby vaporizing the aroma-forming chemicals, enabling the fragrance to travel farther in the air.

Scientists who have studied the makeup of the odor have found it to be a combination of rotting fish, stinky socks, feces, and Limburger cheese (would you believe that my parents used to store Limburger cheese on the stairway to my bedroom when I was a kid?). Add to the mix a cloying sweet floral smell and you've got one amazingly stinky flower!

The blossom usually begins to die back within twelve to twenty-four hours and will remain dormant for a matter of months, until a huge leaf reaching 20 feet tall grows to take its place. The corpse flower won't bloom again until it is able to generate and store adequate energy, which can often take up to seven years. Sadly, the corpse flower isn't hardy enough to grow in our gardens, and attempting it as a houseplant is guaranteed to lead to expensive relationship counseling.

Interestingly, there are a few relatives of the corpse flower that share many of the same exotic characteristics, yet are hardy and generally easy to grow outdoors year-round in the Puget Sound region. Voodoo lily (*Amorphophallus konjac*) is supercool and hardy to about 0 degrees F. It features a fleshy mottled green-and-purple stalk about 4 feet tall, topped by a tropical-looking, heavily cut large leaf.

Eventually, if the voodoo lily stores enough energy, an incredibly stinky vase-shaped 2-foot-tall flower will appear. The blossom is heavily stippled on the outside and shiny lacquered purple within. From the center, a burgundy spadix shoots upward. Hold your nose. The stench is almost as overpowering as that of its bigger cousin! Plant the tubers 4 to 6 inches deep in well-drained, humus-rich soil in an area with early morning sun or partial shade.

After flowering, the plant will rest for a month, or even a year, before it will produce any leaf growth. The tubers cannot withstand saturated conditions, so protect the roots from winter rains by mulching over the roots with a thick cover of water-repellent evergreen fern fronds in fall. If the plant is happy, mother tubers divide, creating big aromatic clumps that will amaze your neighbors in spring.

Another easy-to-grow, equally hardy amorphophallus relative, also commonly called voodoo lily, is *Sauromatum venosum*. In spring, this shade-loving arum from the Himalayas and southern India produces a devilishly attractive flower featuring a foot-long wildly colorful red-, yellow-, and purple-spotted tongue-like extension. The upward-facing maroon spadix resembles a bony finger. Mercifully, the overpowering odor usually lasts for only about four hours. The flower is followed by a spotted stem that grows to 3 or 4 feet tall and forms a heavily cut wide leaf at the top. These easy-to-grow shade lovers also divide regularly to produce large colonies in shady, moist conditions.

Finally, the dragon lily (*Dracunculus vulgaris*) is an amorphophallus relative that often mysteriously shows up in Puget Sound gardens after seed is dropped by birds. Dragon lily is hardy to −20 degrees F, loves morning sun, and will quickly form a clump in well-drained soil. Everything about this plant is exotic. First, a green-and-purple mottled stem that resembles snakeskin grows to 3 feet tall with two or three heavily divided leaves. Then, provided it has stored enough energy, a sinisterly beautiful, hooded, calla lily–like 18-inch-tall dark-purple flower appears in mid- to late June. The dragon lily isn't trying to attract carrion beetles for pollination. This one wants to attract flies, and it smells like a whole herd of cattle died in your backyard. As an added attraction, when it's in bloom, gazillions of flies crowd the air around it.

Unfortunately, this plant has caused me some marital difficulties. Twenty years ago, before I even heard of a dragon lily, a friend stopped by to give me a bulb from this amazing plant, but he wouldn't tell me what it was. He simply told me that I was in for a big surprise when it bloomed. Since I had no idea what it was and feared it might run and take over the garden, I planted it in a confined space back behind the garage. Wouldn't you know it would go and bloom on my mother-in-law's eightieth birthday! Worse yet, my wife, Mary, had invited the family over to celebrate in our back garden.

I was off giving a garden talk and would be home late to join the party. Right before the guests started to arrive, Mary noticed a horrible odor. She thought a raccoon or some other large animal must have died in our backyard. After a search, she discovered that my plant was the culprit. Knowing that I'd never seen it in bloom, she was too nice to cut off the flower, so she moved all of the tables and chairs to the other side of the garden to escape the smell.

Even then, during the party the stench was so strong, every time the wind blew toward the partygoers, they all cussed me out knowing my plant was the cause of the vile odor.

Then, later in the evening, one of Mary's brothers showed up in a taxi. He'd come all the way from North Carolina to surprise his mom on her birthday. They distracted her so he could sneak in and hide, but unfortunately he hid behind the garage. He was supposed to come out shouting "Surprise!" but instead he came out choking and retching, and it took about ten minutes before he could even give her a hug!

All these years later, I still have a huge clump of dragon lily growing in my garden, and several of the plants bloom every year. I did move my dragon lilies, however. They're now planted on the far side of my garden, outside the fence along the sidewalk, where my neighbors get to enjoy the fragrant blooms!

PART 7

Tidbits

A Thorny Dilemma

I'm proud to tell you that I'm one of only two people who have given a talk every year at the Northwest Flower and Garden show since it began in 1989. The first talk I gave was a demonstration on pruning roses. There were no pictures or screens involved. I brought potted-up roses and showed my audience how to prune them.

It was difficult to come up with samples for the talk. I put out a request for roses people no longer wanted. I received plenty of offers, as long as I would dig them up, but most were diseased disasters or huge old behemoths that had not been cared for and thus became too large for the garden. Fortunately, I came up with a few good roses that would work for the talk.

I began with a big English rose that I had dug and potted up from my own garden. The pot was heavy but I managed to drag it to the middle of the stage. In my talk, I told my audience that rose pruning should be done in late February or early March. The goal when pruning tea and English-type roses is to develop an urn-shaped plant. Begin by removing any dead canes. Then remove any sucker growth that comes from below the graft union. Prune the main canes two-thirds of the way to the ground, cutting to an outward-facing bud, and remove dead, weak, or diseased canes. Don't remove too many of the healthy canes. Roses store energy in their stems, so the more canes you keep, the more vigorous the rose.

My next topic was how to prune climbing roses. Once again, begin by removing dead, diseased, dying, and weak shoots, and saw off any dead stumps at the base. Then cut about a third of the oldest canes to the ground. The goal here is to stimulate vigorous new shoots to grow up from the base.

One of the problems with climbing and tall-growing shrub roses is that they tend to form flowering shoots only at the highest point on the cane. To encourage blossoming lower on the plant, tie in the new shoots as horizontally as possible. If the rose is growing against a fence or a wall, pound in horseshoe nails in order to tie in the new canes horizontally. Roses will form all along the cane.

If the rose is growing up a pillar or arbor, twist the pliable new shoots gently around the uprights, keeping the shoots as horizontal as feasible. Blooms usually form at the bends in the canes. Stimulate additional side branching by snipping off the tips of the canes. Hopefully your climbing rose—even old ones that have become overgrown—will reward you by growing plenty of new shoots and flowering like a spring chicken!

The plant I used to demonstrate how to prune climbing roses was huge. It came from the garden of a friend who said I could have it because it had become a crowded mess and sported such nasty prickers, she didn't want to bother renovating it. I managed to dig it out without cutting it back, but after I potted up the monster, it was heavy and difficult to manage. Most of the canes were more than 12 feet long, and it was a real battle getting it onto the stage for my talk.

The real trouble started when I tried to bring it to center stage for the demonstration. The long canes got tangled up with the branches of other roses I had brought. I tugged the pot really hard and the tangled canes pulled free, but they snapped back and hit me right smack in the forehead. It hurt like a beetlehopper, but I tried not to wince and continued with my talk.

To my horror, I felt blood running down my face. I didn't have a handkerchief or tissue, so I stood there bleeding in front of the audience not at all sure what to do. Then a woman sitting in the first row stood up, walked onto the stage, wiped my face with a tissue, and stuck a large Band-Aid on my forehead. Then she walked back and quietly took her seat. I thanked her profusely from the stage, but she just smiled back and never said a thing. After the talk, I was besieged by audience members. By the time I answered all their questions, I went to thank the woman who helped me but she was gone.

I'll probably never know who that person was, but that act of kindness prevented my very first talk at the Northwest Flower and Garden show from ending in disaster and I'll be forever grateful to her!

Everything, Especially Wood Chips, in Moderation

My radio career started in the early 1980s when I received a call from KIRO radio asking me to rush right down to the studio to sub for well-known WSU County Extension Agent George Pinyuh. I was to go on the air with Jim French to answer garden questions, then host George's two-hour question-and-answer garden show.

I was a nervous wreck, as I'd never even been on radio before. As it turned out, I didn't know half the answers to the callers' questions. I said "I don't know" so many times, it became a comedy routine. To my great surprise, listeners called in asking the station to put that oddball gardener on again.

I began to carry a pager and anytime it beeped, it meant that a Mariners game was rained out or ended early. I would run down to the studio to fill in the extra time answering garden questions from callers. One time it went off when my wife, Mary, and I were having dinner at a restaurant, and after I ran out, she overheard diners saying, "That guy must be a very important doctor."

A few months later, George decided to retire from his radio show and I was amazed beyond living tweetle when he recommended me to take his place.

I was thrilled to have my own call-in gardening show, but I was also terrified of making a mistake. That's because when I started hosting the show, I had been a WSU master gardener for only a few years. There were plenty of seasoned master gardeners who would have been happy to take over for George. I felt like everyone I knew, including George, was listening to the show to see if I was the right guy for the job.

That's why I got a bit upset a couple of months into taking over the show when a woman named Mary from Renton called. The first thing she said was, "I want to wring your neck!" My inclination was to hit the hang-up button and say, "Oh, darn, did I lose her?" but I hung in there and asked what I had done to upset her.

She reminded me that she had called in on one of my first shows. Back then, she had asked me if it was really necessary to mulch, and if so, what was the best mulch to use in a mixed border containing a variety of trees, shrubs, and perennials. I had answered that she definitely should mulch her garden every year. Applying a layer of organic mulch on the soil surface can slow evaporation—reducing the need to water as often—help protect roots from winter freezes, suppress weed growth, and reduce compaction and nutrient leaching caused by winter rain pounding bare earth.

I had explained to her that my favorite mulches are compost and arborist wood chips. Compost is the best choice in a garden where plants are frequently moved or replaced, such as in a vegetable or cutting garden. Digging and mixing in compost improves soil structure by increasing organic matter and improving moisture- and nutrient-holding capacities.

In her mixed bed, however, I told her that using arborist wood chips was the best choice. Wood-chip mulch greatly increases populations of beneficial fungi that make soil nutrients more available to woody plants and perennials. Wood chips also encourage beneficial microbes that help suppress soil-borne diseases. A thick layer of wood chips between plants gives very effective weed control, and when applied on a yearly basis, the mix of wood and leaves breaks down to form rich topsoil. When you apply the wood chips, just make sure to avoid buildups around the trunks of trees and shrubs.

The main nuisance with wood chips (or any raw organic substance) is that the chips must be moved out of the way when you're digging or planting. If they get mixed in, microorganisms in the soil rob nutrients in the process of breaking the chips down, and serious nutrient deficiencies can result. However, as long as the wood chips aren't dug in and are used only as a covering on the soil surface, they won't cause deficiencies; nor will they change soil pH.

A major benefit of wood chips is that the arborist is happy to give them away for free; otherwise, he or she has to pay to get rid of them. Hence, on her previous call, I told Mary from Renton that if she saw an arborist at work, to check to see if he or she could deliver some to her house. Evidently, that's exactly what happened. She said her husband was taking a nap before leaving for a business meeting, and she drove off to run some errands.

She hadn't been driving very far when she spotted an arborist running branches through the grinder. She pulled over and checked to see if the chips were fairly uniform. I had advised her to do this because if the blades on the grinder are dull, the wood chips can be stringy and unattractive. The chips looked great, so she asked the arborist to drop a load at her house. Imagine her surprise when she got home three hours later. Her husband was standing next to his car on the other side of a 20-yard-pile of wood chips that were completely blocking the driveway, wondering "Where in the hell did this come from?"

Since she hadn't told the arborist how much she wanted, my guess is that he called a bunch of his buddies to tell them to dump their loads at her house. If you see an arborist at work and ask for wood chips, specify how much you want and where you want it dumped.

The only advice I could think of to give the unfortunate caller was to buy a case of wine and invite all the neighbors over for a party. Then, after most of the neighbors had enjoyed ample libation, give a little talk about the virtues of using wood chips as mulch and let them know that she was more than happy to share. Hopefully, she would get enough of her neighbors excited about mulching to make a significant dent in the pile. I never did find out if her husband managed to get his car out of the driveway!

Alfalfa Meal: A "Swell" Fertilizer

I feed many of the plants in my garden regularly. Fertilizing provides the nutrition needed for strong growth. It also encourages repeat bloomers such as clematis, dahlias, scabiosa, roses, torch lilies, et cetera, to produce beautiful blooms all summer long. My favorite fertilizer is a mixture of alfalfa meal and organic flower food. Alfalfa meal is cram-packed with growth regulators and hormones that tell your plant "Bloom, you fool, bloom," while organic flower food provides additional nutrients and minerals necessary for healthy growth.

As a general guideline, around the average-size tea rose apply 2 cups of alfalfa meal combined with the recommended rate of organic fertilizer. Make the first application when the first new leaves appear in spring. Perennials that bloom only once per season, such as peony, generally require only one application in March or early April. To keep repeat bloomers flowering away, apply the above recipe about once every six weeks starting in March or early April through the end of August.

If you aren't familiar with alfalfa meal, there are some tips to be aware of. First of all, hold your breath or wear a bandanna when you apply it. The meal is dusty, and as I found out, breathing it can clog up your lungs for a few days.

Also, be aware that alfalfa meal is fairly alkaline, so avoid applying it to acid-loving plants such as rhododendrons, camellias, and blueberries. Don't make the mistake I did of applying it to a blue-flowering hydrangea. Hydrangea flowers become pinker in alkaline soil. After I worked alfalfa meal into the soil around my 'Blue Wave' hydrangea, the previously sparkling-blue flowers turned the ugliest mauve I've ever seen.

Store the bag of alfalfa meal in a metal can. I didn't in the beginning, and every mouse in Western Washington spent the night in my garage enjoying a gourmet feast. There was mouse poop from one end of the garage to the other and I was banned from brussels sprouts casseroles for a month afterward.

Fortunately, alfalfa meal does not attract rodents once it's worked into the soil. It works better mixed in as well, so when you apply it, use a hoe or other tool to work it into the soil around the plant.

Finally, because buying a small container of alfalfa meal at a quality nursery can be a bit expensive, you can save money by purchasing it at a feed store where it is often available in bulk as horse feed. If they offer alfalfa only in pellet form, it's fine to use as long as it doesn't contain mineral supplements for rabbits, because those additives might be harmful to plants.

If you use the straight alfalfa pellets, break them down first. In the evening before you plan to use them, fill a normal-size bucket one-third full with the pellets and then fill the bucket with water. In the morning, the bucket will be filled with alfalfa schluck. You can apply it at the same rate as you would the meal. One advantage of using the schluck is that it isn't dusty, so you don't have to hold your breath while applying it.

If you don't turn the pellets into schluck, you may have troubles as I learned when a professional gardener called to warn listeners on my radio show. The caller said she was using the pellets to fertilize the plants in a client's garden, but at that time she was unaware of the need to turn the pellets into schluck. Instead she spread the untreated pellets around the various plants, planning to come back at the end to work them all in. I didn't see the harm in this. I figured the only problem was that the pellets would have taken longer to break down, and therefore the feeding might not have been as effective.

The caller said that wasn't the problem. Instead, what happened was that the people who owned the garden had two young golden Labs. When the gardener was almost done spreading the pellets, she suddenly realized the dogs had been following behind, eating them practically as fast as she had been putting them out.

When I asked if it harmed the pups, she said it didn't harm them, but it made them really thirsty. When she gave them a drink, as she described it, suddenly they were "twice the pups they used to was!"

So definitely make the pellets into schluck before putting it around your plants, and don't forget to work it in. Even without dogs, you don't want a bunch of swelled-up raccoons, squirrels, and mice running around your garden!

Eau de Vinegar

One thing that I enjoy about my radio show is the exchange of gardening information with listeners. Although I am supposed to be the garden expert giving advice, I often learn new tips from radio listeners. Years ago, a caller asked me what type of weed and feed he should use to kill the dandelions in his lawn. I told him that I never use chemical weed-and-feed products because of possible health risk to children and pets. Instead, I recommended a method that I used on dandelions in my own lawn back then.

It was a tool that I nicknamed the "grandpa weeding tool," because the old guy who sold it to me at a garage sale looked just like my grandpa Waldo. It has a long handle and a footrest that you step on over the weed. Then you pull the handle toward you, and underground clasps grab the root and pop the weed out of the ground.

At the time, it was the only nonchemical method of lawn-weed control I knew of, but I had to admit that I wasn't crazy about using the tool. It was a lot of work, left my lawn full of unsightly holes, and often broke the root off underground. When that happens, the weed doesn't just grow back: it usually doubles and you get two dandelions for the price of one. After I described the "grandpa weeding tool," the caller said he would try it, but I could sense some hesitation on his part.

The next caller was an older woman who had been gardening for a long time. In reference to the previous caller, she asked me, "Haven't you heard about using vinegar to kill weeds?" When I admitted ignorance, I received quite a lecture on why and how to use vinegar as a weed control, but I'm glad I did. I've been using it ever since, and it quickly became the only weed control I used at Seattle University and at home.

Over the years, I've experimented with different methods of applying it, but the advice she gave me was generally quite accurate. Buy straight white vinegar from the grocery store. It's safe for the environment, people, and pets, yet it will kill practically any weed. Stronger pickling vinegars are available, but I find that straight white vinegar works just as well on all but the most stubborn weeds.

Don't dilute the vinegar by adding water. Also, be aware that it works well only on a hot, sunny day with temperatures in the high 70s or above. The hotter and sunnier the weather, the better it works. Vinegar will kill most any plant it hits. I suspect it changes the soil pH, so it probably isn't a good idea to spray over the root zone of valued plants. I don't recommend using it in a mixed border or in a vegetable garden.

To keep my lawn dandelion-free, I apply vinegar once in spring and follow up with another treatment in fall. The only problem is that vinegar also kills any grass you hit when you're spraying the weed. To minimize collateral damage, I use a sprayer with a long spray wand. I unscrew the nozzle from the end of the wand, slip a funnel onto the wand, and duct-tape it on before replacing the nozzle. Then I place the funnel over the weed and against the ground, thereby greatly reducing overspray.

Don't be dainty with the vinegar. The first time I tried using it, I sprayed sparingly and it didn't work. The next time I gave each weed a heavy dose and it worked like a charm. Within about three hours the dandelions and other broad-leaved weeds that had been sprayed were brown and dead as a doornail, and they never grew back. It worked so fast, it reminded me of when the Wicked Witch of the West in *The Wizard of Oz* got doused with water. You could almost hear the weeds shout, "*I'm melting, I'm melting!*"

Even with the funnel on the end of the spray wand, you usually end up with a circular 4-to-6-inch spot of dead grass where you sprayed out a weed. Wait a few days after spraying to allow the effect of the vinegar to dissipate. Then use a large screwdriver or hand weeding tool to punch holes in the lawn and drop grass seed directly into the holes. Grass seed that germinates on the soil surface usually won't survive because the thatch buildup is too thick for roots to gain a foothold, whereas grass that germinates in the holes almost always thrives. Apply organic lawn food and keep the soil surface moist. Within three weeks, the grass will fill in and you won't know you ever had a dead spot.

It's best to treat lawn weeds with vinegar when the grass is actively growing. I do it on the first warm sunny day in March or April and again in mid- to late September. Visitors to our garden are always amazed that my lawn is dandelion-free, especially considering that my neighbor's lawn resembles a dandelion farm.

I don't use vinegar to kill only weeds in my lawn, by the way. I find it's equally effective as Roundup when used on weeds growing in sidewalk cracks or on gravel driveways. Since there is no lawn to worry about killing, you can use vinegar on sidewalks and gravel all summer long.

At Seattle University, we used vinegar to kill weeds growing in cracks on a stairway, and to our surprise, it killed the moss as well. After that, we used vinegar to control moss on any hard surface where it was a problem. Just as with weeds, it works best on moss when temperatures are in the high 70s or above.

Having raved about the effectiveness of vinegar, I need to add a warning here. If you have a hot date planned for an evening after spraying vinegar, make sure it's someone who likes pickles. After a hard day of spraying, you're going to be wearing "eau de gherkin" for the next four days!

Mollusk Marauders

I grew up in Wisconsin, where the few slugs we had were tiny and did little damage. That's why I was so amazed when I moved to Seattle. According to *The Secret World of Slugs and Snails* by David George Gordon, there are at least thirty-three different kinds of snails and slugs in the Pacific Northwest, and they come in a wide variety of shapes and sizes. I still remember when I saw my first banana slug. It was at least 8 inches long, bright yellow with black spots.

Actually, what I really remember is how slimy and gooey it felt when I accidentally stepped on one barefoot in the middle of the night on a camping trip!

It didn't take me long to understand why most Northwest gardeners hate slugs and snails. It's hard to like slimy creatures that can be so damaging to both edible plants and prized orna-mentals. There's a reason these mollusks are so destructive. Slugs and snails typically have more than 20,000 teeth. They eat several times their body weight every day and are capable of traveling up to 40 feet in a single night in search of food.

Slugs and snails also build up quite large populations. Studies have shown that there can be as many as 6,000 slugs in the aver-age Northwest garden in spring—and that's not even counting the snails. They have both male and female reproductive organs and are capable of mating with themselves if necessary. The oval eggs are laid in clutches of 30 to 50 eggs at a time. Most slugs lay at least 200 eggs per year, but the brown garden snail can lay up to as many as 500 in one season.

Most of us rely on slug bait as a critical tool in the battle to protect vulnerable plants. The newer iron phosphate–based slug baits such as Sluggo, Worry Free, and Escar-Go! are effective and significantly safer to use around pets and children than are the ones that contain metaldehyde. One year, a saleswoman at the Northwest Flower and Garden show was actually eating the newer bait to show people how safe it is. (Now that I think about it, I haven't seen her since then. . . .)

Just the same, use all slug bait with caution. A recent study found that even these newer slug baits can be harmful to dogs if eaten in quantity. Follow label directions carefully, and store these products in a secure location where pets and children can't reach them.

There are other effective nontoxic methods to help control slugs and snails. A natural solution that is 100 percent effective is to install a 3-inch-wide barrier of copper foil (available at quality nurseries) on the sides of raised beds and containers. Slugs and snails won't cross the barrier because the movement of their stomach muscles combined with their slime creates an electrical charge on the copper. It's fun to see the look in their beady little eyes when they get the shock!

You can also entice slugs for a last drink at "Slimy's Saloon" by putting out cottage-cheese containers filled with ½ inch of beer. Slugs and snails are party animals, and their love for beer can be used to our advantage. The mollusks drink too much, become anesthetized, and drown. Any tub-shaped 16-ounce container will work as a beer trap, but I prefer clear plastic containers because they don't show up as much in the garden. Cut four equally spaced 1-inch-square holes in the rim of the container—these are the slug doors. Then fill with beer and put the lid on because it will keep the rain and sprinklers from diluting the beer. More importantly, it will also keep your pooch from becoming a beeraholic. When I noticed my dog was smiling funny, I actually had to put a heavy rock on top of the beer trap to keep her on the wagon.

There are a few things to know in order to use beer traps effectively. As far as slugs and snails are concerned, all beers are not equal. I've done empirical studies in my back garden, and some beers are much more attractive than others. I used to use an inexpensive beer called Heidelberg. The slugs and snails were so crazy about that stuff, you could actually hear them yodel when you put it out in the garden. Heidelberg beer is no longer available, but I've found that Bud Light works very well. You might want to do your own test to find a cheap beer that slugs and snails can't resist.

In order to be successful, you need to entice these destructive critters to go to happy hour before they go to the restaurant. If they stop for dinner on the way to the tavern, it could be disastrous for some of your favorite plants. Place at least three beer traps around any susceptible plant that you are trying to protect so that the mollusks will be attracted to the beer first and stop in for a (last) drink before dinner.

The amount of beer required in the trap changes as summer progresses. In spring you generally need only about ½ inch of beer. At that time, most slugs and snails are recently hatched and are small. However, they keep growing all season and can become quite large. I watched a 6-inch-long slug drink all the beer in a trap before staggering off into the bushes to sleep it off, only to return the next night to do more damage. Up the ante as summer progresses to make sure there is ample beer to do in the bigger ones.

Beer traps also need to be emptied on a regular basis. Once there are about five partygoers in a typical trap, potential patrons look in the entrance, decide it isn't their kind of establishment, and hit the road.

Whenever there are about five slugs or snails in the tavern, dig a good-size hole, toss the beer in with the partygoers, and cover them with dirt. Keep filling the hole in this way until it is the right depth to plant a shrub or perennial. I don't know if it's the beer, the slugs, or the symbiotic relationship, but beer and mollusks make great fertilizer. Your plant will grow like crazy.

There is one other thing to remember when you are using beer traps to catch slugs and snails. Place the container on the ground. Don't use the often-recommended method of burying an open-top beer trap so that the top is level with the soil surface. If you do, you're liable to catch "eek-squish" bugs. They are the big iridescent beetles that come running out when you pick up a rock or a piece of wood in the garden. They're actually called carabid or ground beetles, but they've been nicknamed "eek-squish" bugs because when folks see them, they scream and stomp on them.

Those beetles have bad breath because they eat slugs and snails! Most beetle varieties eat only the eggs and newly hatched slugs and snails, but there is one very streamlined chestnut-brown beetle variety called the slug/snail destroyer that will take on full-grown mollusks. You haven't lived until you see a beetle devour a 5-inch slug in the night! These beetles are not attracted to beer, but they may not notice the buried traps and fall in. I once found forty dead carabid beetles in a bucket buried level as an open-topped beer trap. That's a lot of good guys that would have been eating slugs and snails.

By the way, there are a number of animals besides "eek-squish" bugs that eat slugs and snails. Toads are known to eat them, and if you're lucky enough to have garter snakes hiding out in your garden, you definitely won't have a slug or snail problem. Chickens devour them and raccoons feast on them as well. There are even snails that eat slugs and other snails. Unfortunately, those snails also eat our plants, so they don't do much good.

Ducks are also renowned for gobbling up slugs, but don't try feeding one to a duck. I learned that lesson when I was visiting a friend who raised ducks in Oregon. I really wanted to see a duck eat a slug, so when I found a really big one, my friend said I could feed it to her duck. The problem was that the slug rolled up into a tight ball in my hand and when the duck tried to eat it, she choked on it. The duck started running in circles, flapping her wings and making an awful gagging quacking noise. Thank goodness she somehow managed to swallow it. I thought I was going to have to perform a Heimlich maneuver on a duck. By the way, I don't know if ducks eat snails, but I'm definitely not going to feed one to a duck to find out!

Finally, there is one animal that eats the highly destructive brown garden snail found in most of our gardens. These snails are the same as the ones they serve as escargot in France. They were introduced to this country in the 1800s when a French restaurateur brought them over, thinking that Americans would develop a taste for them. We didn't, but the snails escaped and quickly developed a taste for our plants. They've eaten their way up West Coast gardens all the way into Canada. Fortunately, there is an effective biological control. Just convince lots of French people to move into your neighborhood!

Fences Make for Good Neighbors

I'm not a fan of hedges, especially ones made up of only one type of plant. In the first place, a standard evergreen hedge requires too much maintenance. You'll spend half your life shearing it to keep it tidy and within bounds. Even worse, a large grouping of the same plant could attract harmful insects or be susceptible to disease.

In my opinion, if you want a hedge, a better choice is to plant what the English call a mixed hedgerow. These are hedges made up of an assortment of evergreen and deciduous trees and shrubs that require similar growing conditions. Mixed hedgerows provide food and nesting sites for a wide variety of birds, and they tend to attract beneficial insects that, in turn, disperse throughout the garden to feed on harmful ones. They are also less likely to be plagued by insect pests and disease.

Maintenance in a mixed hedgerow is greatly reduced as well. The key is to select trees and shrubs whose maximum height and width are the same as the desired dimensions of the hedgerow. Then, other than removal of a wayward or damaged branch, your mixed hedgerow should require minimal pruning.

To create your mixed hedgerow, begin by strategically locating taller-growing broad-leaved evergreens and conifers where they are needed to provide privacy. Some of my favorite taller-growing evergreens include *Arbutus unedo* (strawberry tree), *Calocedrus decurrens* (incense cedar), *Chamaecyparis obtusa* (hinoki false cypress), *Myrica californica* (Pacific wax myrtle), rhamnus (buck-thorn), and thuja (arborvitae). Avoid the popular, very fast-growing × *Cuprocyparis leylandii* (Leyland cypress). They look great when you plant them but soon lose their attractive shape and are suscep-tible to disease. With the larger plants in place, fill in the gaps with an assortment of lower-growing deciduous and evergreen trees or shrubs. Look for plants with colorful foliage, flowers, showy fruit and berries, and varying texture. Closer spacing will fill in more quickly, but allow sufficient space for the plants to maintain their natural form.

In truth, however, I prefer fences when it comes to providing privacy. Fences are aesthetically pleasing and make a wonderful backdrop for trees, shrubs, and flowering plants. They play a practical role by keeping your dog in the yard. In deer country, fences keep little Bambi out of the garden, as long as they are at least 6 feet tall. Best of all, fences never require pruning, need little maintenance, and when they wear out, can easily be replaced with minimal disruption to the garden.

Fences are often works of art in their own right. There is a fence design for every garden theme. Bamboo fencing or a fence with a bamboo design contributes to an Asian theme in the garden. Wrought-iron fences are best suited for a formal garden. White picket fences are a bit high-maintenance but create a country gar-den feel and give a sense of enclosure while allowing open views into the garden. Artistic fence gates are also becoming popular. They add spice to the garden and let visitors know that they are entering a special place.

There are professional fence builders who design and build superb fences that will add real pizzazz to your garden, but it's not that difficult to build one yourself. I'm a horrible carpenter, but I managed to build a nice, albeit simple, cedar fence for my garden. The seasoned wood serves as the perfect backdrop for my mixed beds and gives us privacy in our urban backyard. I recommend spacing the slats about ⅛ inch apart. Slight spacing gives the wood room to flex; it also allows air to flow through the fence without sacrificing privacy. Airflow is important to help prevent fungus diseases, such as black spot on rose and botrytis on peony.

I've seen a lot of fence designs that I admire, but I'll never forget quite an unusual one I came across while attending a local garden tour. It was an attractive 6-foot-tall newly constructed cedar fence with a lattice top. It extended from the back of the house to the end of the property. Obviously designed for privacy, the fence was constructed with minimal space between the slats. There was, however, something odd about this fence. The section by the patio, where the homeowners dined regularly, had big open spaces that allowed the neighbors to look right in. I couldn't imagine why it was designed that way, unless the folks who lived there had a really close friendship with their neighbors and liked to talk with them while they were enjoying their dinner.

When I asked the homeowner about the design, he told me that they had recently removed a ratty old hedge, and other than improving the appearance of the garden, one of the main reasons they had the fence constructed was to give them more privacy. When they had the fence built, however, they forgot about the much-beloved neighbor dog, who made a habit of coming through the hedge to join them for dinner in order to enjoy a few table scraps. The first time they dined after the new fence was built, they heard their old friend crying on the other side of the fence. They felt so bad, they had the fence company come back and rebuild the patio section with gaps to allow Fido to stick his snout through so he could join them for dinnertime snacks again. Let's face it: there are things in life way more important than privacy!

Scientific Inquiry Has Its Limitations

When it comes to gardening, nothing is more important than the soil, and one of the keys to knowing the quality of soil is how well it drains. Fortunately, there's an easy test you can use to find that out. I've used this method to test drainage countless times over the years.

To test drainage, dig a 1-foot-square hole 1 foot deep. If you are testing a large area, you may want to dig a few holes. Fill the hole with water right to the top. Then measure how much water drains in one hour.

If the water level went down between 1 and 3 inches, you've got great well-draining soil and you'll be able to grow practically any kind of garden plant with average drainage needs. If you are putting in a new landscape with a blank canvas, till in compost before you plant. Adding compost improves soil structure and adds moisture- and nutrient-holding capacity. It also introduces a wide variety of beneficial microorganisms that help keep disease organisms in check. Generally it's best if the makeup of most soils is about one-third organic. For example, if you apply 2 inches of compost on the surface, till it 6 inches deep into the existing soil.

If the water in the test hole drains more than 4 inches per hour, your soil is too sandy. Up the ante by tilling in a 3-inch layer of compost 6 inches deep. That will add 50 percent organic compost to the mix, which will greatly improve moisture- and nutrient-holding capacities. Mulching the surface heavily on a yearly basis will also help slow evaporation, reducing the need to water as often.

Finally, if the water in the test hole drains less than 1 inch per hour, drainage is poor and you'll be able to grow only a limited amount of plants in that soil. You're most likely dealing with clay or hardpan, and adding compost won't solve your problem. There are two ways to deal with poorly drained soil. The least-expensive way is to choose plants that evolved in, and therefore thrive in, poorly drained soils. An excellent book that lists plants that thrive in poor drainage is *Right Plant, Right Place* by Nicola Ferguson. It is also an excellent reference for other difficult situations such as dry shade, et cetera. If you want to have vastly more choice when it comes to planting, the other, albeit more-expensive, solution is to bring in manufactured topsoil to create berms or raised beds. As long as you raise the soil level enough to allow two-thirds of a plant's roots to remain above the clay or hardpan, as well as making sure the berm is wide enough to allow for adequate root growth, most any plant will flourish.

There are a number of ways to create raised beds that are attractive and fit into the landscape. At Seattle University, in areas with drainage issues, we used large outcropping stones to help hold the soil, then planted conifers and rock-garden plants to create an attractive alpine look. These berms must have looked quite natural, because campus visitors often asked me if they were created by glacial activity. Berms drain quickly, so mulch yearly to prevent having to water too frequently.

As simple as my drainage test is to perform, things can go wrong. WSU County Extension Agent George Pinyuh convinced me to help him install a landscape for his friend, who had just bought a newly constructed home. I packed up my large hound dog Goldie, who went everywhere with me, and headed for the job site.

The plan was for me to start by tilling in a layer of compost. We would begin planting the chosen trees and shrubs as soon as George arrived. In the meantime, I spread the compost and fired up the tiller. When I flipped the lever to activate the tines, however, the machine took off like a roadrunner. The soil was so hard, it was like trying to till concrete. I practically went right through the side of the house!

I immediately called George and told him that the soil was terrible and that we either had to build berms or choose different plants. George disagreed. He said he knew the soil in that area, and the problem was caused by the bulldozers and other construction equipment driving over and compacting the soil. He said that once I was able to break through the surface with the tiller, it would drain perfectly well.

I had definite doubts, so we made another of my famous high-stakes bets. We'd do the drain test and whoever was wrong had to buy a cookie for the winner.

As soon as I started digging the hole, I knew I was going to win. The hardpan was so dense, digging in it practically broke my arm. As soon as George arrived, we filled the hole with water, set a stopwatch, and went off to work. I couldn't wait for the hour to end, sure that I would be claiming victory.

When we returned an hour later, to my great surprise and chagrin, the water level had dropped more than 4 inches. George was strutting around like a peacock, bragging about being the soil expert and rubbing in how good the cookie was going to taste. Then the woman next door who had been watching me work all morning called out to me.

"Sir," she said, "that water didn't drain."

When I asked what she meant, she said, "Your dog drank that water!"

Pay attention when you do a test like this. Unexpected events can surely happen!

PART 8

Travel Adventures

The Origin of Oh, La La

Everywhere I go, people ask me why I say "oh, la la" so often. By the way, it's not "ooh, la la," as people often think. It's a French term, but it's pronounced "oh, la la" and indicates a fairly strong reaction to something that was just said or done. I began using the phrase after an experience I had on one of our many visits to France.

My wife, Mary, and I are avid travelers. One of our favorite jobs is hosting garden tours to countries around the world. At this writing, we've led seventeen excursions to Europe and beyond. We also travel on our own, however, and most of those trips involve some kind of strenuous activity such as long hikes or bike rides.

One particularly memorable trip was when just the two of us hiked the entire length of the French Alps on the Grande Randonnée Cinq (GR5). The famous trail is about 360 miles long, and we're still arguing over whether it took twenty-eight or twenty-nine days to complete. We began the hike by dipping our hands in Lake Geneva and finished by wading into the Mediterranean. The ending was even more exciting than we thought it would be as it ended on a nude beach!

During our twenty-eight days (or twenty-nine, depending on who you talk to), we stayed in mountain huts, so we had to carry only our clothes, personal items, and a sleeping sheet. The huts provided beds, blankets, and meals. Despite the good food and comfortable beds, the hiking was demanding. The GR5 trail winds its way down through towns at the base of a mountain, up and over steep passes, and finally climbs to the next hut, usually situated near or at the top of another mountain. When we finally arrived at a hut after a hard day of hiking, the first thing I always muttered was, *"Je voudrais un vin rouge s'il vous plaît"* (I'd like a red wine please). It's great for pain!

Every mountain hut is different. Some hold scores of hikers, while others have room for only around twelve people. You don't get much privacy and often sleep in a room with six or more strangers, but that's just part of the experience. By far the most interesting hut we stayed in was a big building with a 50-foot mattress running right through the middle of it. The madame in charge showed us where we were to sleep, and we realized we had no idea who we would be sleeping next to on the mattress.

In the middle of the night, I woke up with my arm around Mary. Then I thought, *Which side is Mary on?* Thank goodness I didn't have my arm around Jacques!

My penchant for the phrase "oh, la la" came from a 1,000-mile bicycle trip Mary and I ventured on in France. We started in southern Provence and rode about 60 miles a day, until we ended at a friend's house in Bretagne in northwestern France. We carried our tent, sleeping bags, and everything else we needed on our bikes and stayed in French campgrounds.

We were riding in an area near Aix-en-Provence when we spotted something brand-new to us. It was a bathroom shaped like a big plastic igloo. If you've been in France in the last twenty years, you've undoubtedly seen them, but they were a new feature at that time and we had never seen one before.

We recognized what is was, so we pulled over. I sat on the bench watching our bikes while Mary deposited the required two francs and went in. In a few minutes she came out, holding the door saying, "You won't believe it in there. It's spotlessly clean and it plays great music!"

I jumped up and started fishing in my pockets for a couple of francs when Mary said, "Why waste two francs? I've got the door open; just go in and use it."

I thought, *Yeah, why waste two francs?* I entered and shut the door.

There was, however, one thing we didn't know about these French toilets: they're self-cleaning. When the door shuts, it means the person who used it has left and it's time to clean.

I had just walked up to the front when a jet of soapy water blasted me right in the chest. I ran backward, only to get blasted from behind. I ran for the door. It was locked, and there were jets blasting away from the sides as well. From the bench where she was waiting, Mary was amazed to see the toilet rocking wildly and to hear shrieks coming from within.

Finally the jets stopped, the door opened, and I came staggering out drenched from head to foot—and practically ran into an old French man wearing a beret and holding a baguette. He looked at me and said, "Oh, la la!"

By the way, unless you're in serious need of a shower, I *strongly* recommend putting the coins in the slot before you enter a French toilet!

Himalayan Poppies Will Give You the Blues

I've had the good fortune to be invited to speak in Alaska many times. My first talk was at a garden conference in Juneau about twenty years ago. The capital city of Alaska is beautiful, but it has one of the most unusual gardening climates I've ever experienced. The city is built on the side of the slopes of Mount Roberts and Mount Juneau, and the climate zones on the same street can vary from Zone 7 at the edge of the sea to Zone 4 at the top of the hill.

My talk was geared to gardeners in Southeast Alaska, from Juneau to other coastal cities. Summers there are typically cool and cloudy, while winters are generally windy and rainy, although the ground almost always freezes during the winter months.

My wife, Mary, accompanied me to the conference. Had we known how difficult it could be to fly to Juneau in those days, she might have skipped the trip. The city is surrounded by mountains, it is often foggy, and the plane has to circle a mountain on the approach to the runway. The flight was spectacularly beautiful with magnificent mountain scenery all the way, but as we approached Juneau we saw only mountaintops sticking out of a thick cloud cover. The pilot came on the intercom to tell us to hold on tight as he was going to give landing a try.

We descended into the clouds, but the cover only seemed to get thicker the farther down we went. All of a sudden the engines began to roar, the plane began to rattle and shake, and we were thrown back in our seats as the plane went into a steep climb. It didn't help to hear Mary shouting, "We're going up! We're going up!"

When we popped back above the clouds, the captain came back on the intercom to offer everyone a free drink. Then he told us that it was too risky to try to land in Juneau and we were diverted to Yakutat, a small fishing village to the northwest.

The jet landed in Yakutat problem-free and we were told that our flight to Juneau would take off in four hours. An incredibly friendly man who called himself the "Yakutat Tourist Welcoming Committee" asked us if we would like to see a bit of the region. He took us out in his Jeep to a river where we watched hundreds of eagles feeding on salmon. Evidently he enjoyed meeting strangers and did this whenever a jet was diverted to Yakutat.

When we returned to the airport to board the plane, I got a bad surprise. The woman I was sitting next to asked me how many days I'd been trying to get to Juneau. She said this was her third day of flying back and forth from Seattle to Yakutat because the plane hadn't been able to land in Juneau! By pure luck, the clouds cleared. You've never heard a louder cheer from the passengers than when the jet landed in Juneau that afternoon.

The garden conference was a weekend event and included a tour of some of Juneau's most attractive gardens. There was, however, one unexpected glitch. The winter in Juneau had been unusually sunny and cold, and the ground had not come out of its winter freeze. In a typical year, warm April rains thaw the soil, and by the time the conference is held in May, the gardens have come to life. It became hilarious as every garden we visited consisted of a bunch of leafless dead-looking sticks from even deader-looking perennials. A few gardens had a smattering of hardy rhododendrons, azaleas, bare-stemmed Japanese maples, and dwarf conifers, but for the most part they looked like frozen tundra.

Surprisingly, though, there was one perennial blooming away, and it made me and the other non-Alaskans practically cry with envy. In almost every garden, there were spectacular drifts of Himalayan blue poppies in full flower. No plant can match the elegance and grace of the magnificent Himalayan blue poppy (Meconopsis). There are several species, each with varying shapes and sizes, but generally they are cloaked in attractive silvery-green foliage covered with golden bristles. In spring or early summer, a tall stem appears topped with silky 4-inch-wide iridescent blue blossoms centered with a burst of golden stamens.

It's practically impossible to get these poppies to survive more than one season in Pacific Northwest gardens or basically anywhere else in the continental United States. Evidently the climate in Southeast Alaska is perfect for growing these gorgeous plants. Most of the gardeners there told us that they planted only a few of the poppies, but they readily self-sow to form huge patches within only a couple of years. Everyone was so smitten with the blooming poppies, it didn't matter that they were the only plant flowering. To everyone on the tour, those gardens were gorgeous.

Blue poppies are difficult to grow because, in most climates, they almost always die after flowering. To grow successfully, these picky perennials must have cool, bright shady growing conditions and humus-rich soil. The soil must be kept constantly moist during the growing season, but it also must be extremely well drained. Blue poppies can survive the winter in the frozen soil of Southeast Alaska, but in the rainy Pacific Northwest, unless the drainage is almost perfect, soggy winter conditions inevitably lead to root rot.

A few species, such as Meconopsis 'Lingholm', Meconopsis betonicifolia, and Meconopsis × sheldonii appear to be the most reliable varieties for Northwest gardens, but even those will rarely survive more than one season.

To keep them alive, the first season after planting, you have to pick off the buds to divert the plant's energy from flowering to vegetative growth, in the hopes that it will encourage additional crowns to form. Picking off the flower buds before they open is torturous, because the plant usually ends up dying anyway and then you never even get to see them bloom! I've tried removing the flower buds several times and it has yet to work for me. Evidently, if you have the perfect conditions for growing them and can get them through the first year alive, they might self-sow and become a permanent attraction in your garden. There are a number of Northwest public gardens that have established blue poppy beds. Even in those gardens, however, the head gardeners have confessed that they grow backup plants from seed and overwinter them in greenhouses in order to supplement the clumps, which tend to thin out over time.

If you want to have spectacular blue poppies blooming in your garden, you really have only two choices. Either buy new starts every spring or move to Juneau, where they grow like weeds. If your airplane can get there, that is!

Mystery in the Garden

I frequently host international garden tours, a job I love! Besides having fun and making new friends, we learn about garden design, plants, and plant care by visiting some of the best public and private gardens in the world. Of course, on my tours we also visit sights other than gardens in order to gain an appreciation for the rich culture, history, and scenery and to get to know the lively and colorful locals who inhabit the country.

To enhance the learning experience, I try to make sure that the garden owner or the head gardener is available to lead us through the garden. That way, he or she not only can identify rare and unusual plants and explain the design, but also bring the garden to life by describing its history, often including interesting and sometimes shocking stories about the intrigues and scandals that occurred within the walls of the gardens.

Although we see a lot of famous public gardens on these tours, we also seek out well-known small private gardens. All of our garden visits are carefully planned out well in advance of the tour. However, one of my favorite memories happened after we stopped for lunch in a small town. An older local woman overheard that I was leading a garden tour and wanted to know if we would like to see her garden. She lived right down the street. I could tell she was a character, so I happily accepted the opportunity.

She had, however, one condition we all had to agree to before she would show us her garden. We had to promise that no one would look at her "smalls" that were hanging on the clothesline. I had no idea what smalls were, so she whispered in my ear that they were her underknickers.

I told everyone what the conditions were, and we promised not to peek at the knickers. Of course, you know what happens when someone tells you not to look at something. She probably had a beautiful garden, but I suspect the only thing most of us remember about her garden is those knickers hanging on the clothesline!

That event happened on a trip to southern England. It's said that English people are born with a trowel in their hand, and judging from how many spectacular gardens we saw there, I suspect it's true. We visited some of the world's most famous gardens, including Sissinghurst, Exbury, and Kew, but one of my favorite visits was to the private garden of Lady Kitchener. I'll never know how we managed to get permission to visit the garden of this esteemed member of the English aristocracy. She lived in a lovely cottage that once belonged to Florence Nightingale. It had a thatched roof divided into undulating segments, and the gardens were laid out to match the design of the roof.

Lady Kitchener was a keen gardener. Her garden was full of spectacular combinations of rare and unusual plants. She began the tour of her garden by immediately giving me a plant identification test right in front of everyone on the tour. I felt put on the spot, but by pure miracle I knew the name of every plant she asked about. It impressed the living tweetle out of everyone in my group, including Lady Kitchener herself.

One of the key lessons I've learned from being a gardener is how important soil is when it comes to growing healthy, thriving plants. Soil conditions can vary throughout the garden. If a tree or shrub isn't doing well, it could be a sign that the soil is of poor quality. Sometimes it's because a leaking fuel tank had to be excavated, or a huge stump was removed, and the empty space was filled with less-than-ideal soil. If the soil held too much moisture, was too sandy, or contained toxic substances, any plant growing there would suffer the consequences.

Lady Kitchener had a similar situation in her garden. About halfway through the tour, she showed us a scrawny and somewhat ailing willow-leaved pear (*Pyrus salicifolia*), while neighboring trees and shrubs only a few yards away were healthy and vigorous. Willow-leaved pears are deciduous trees that normally grow 18 feet tall and 12 feet wide and are quite attractive with glossy, willow-like silver-gray leaves. The one in Lady Kitchener's garden was only 6 feet tall. The foliage was sparse, dull, and slightly drooping.

Lady Kitchener told us that when she moved into the house years earlier, the tree had looked exactly the same. She was determined to improve the condition of the tree, but feeding with special fertilizers, careful watering, and even talking to it had no effect. Despite her best efforts, the size and appearance of the tree remained the same.

One day when she was out gardening, she happened to voice her frustration about the tree to one of her neighbors. He had a hunch about what the cause might be and came over to see it.

As soon as the neighbor saw where it was, he said, "There's a Messerschmitt in there."

He told her that, during World War II, a dogfight had occurred in the sky right over her house. A Messerschmitt was shot down and landed in the spot right where the pear was now planted. When it crashed, the plane evidently made a huge hole in the garden and the authorities sent a crew over to fill it in with gravel, covering the Messerschmitt in the process. Then, long before Lady Kitchener moved in, someone planted the ill-fated silver pear in that spot.

So if you have an area of the garden where plants just won't grow well, dig some holes to see what the soil is like. It just might turn out that you have a Messerschmitt in your garden!

I should add that Lady Kitchener (despite the plant ID test she gave me) turned out to be quite a kind and generous host. At the end of the tour, she invited the whole group of us into her gorgeous home and served us tea and biscuits. The only glitch was that one of the people in my tour group spilled a full cup of tea on an antique rug that I suspect was worth at least twice the value of my home.

When I told Lady Kitchener what had happened, she was more than gracious and wasn't put out at all, explaining it would be easy to remove the stain. Her two wiener dogs, Fudge and Toffee, were not so gracious. As Lady Kitchener walked us out to our bus, she was cradling the two dogs in her arms. When I reached out to try to pet them, I almost lost two fingers!

Speaking of fingers, as I was getting on the bus, Lady Kitchener told me she had to hurry back into the house to clean her nails. She was about to go have tea with the queen and didn't want to keep her waiting!

The Naughty Norwegian Princess

When you travel on an international garden tour, you not only see some of the world's most famous gardens, you also meet the world's most renowned gardeners as well. Actually, I should say that you *might* get to meet them. The people who own famous gardens are in such demand, it can be quite pricey to schedule a group tour with them.

I learned that lesson when I was setting up my first tour to England. I hoped that Christopher Lloyd, well-known garden author and owner of the famous Great Dixter, would give us a tour. I realized this would take some luck and could be quite expensive, but I knew he was good friends with my equally famous friend and plant explorer Dan Hinkley, so I did a bit of shameless name-dropping in my e-mail request.

My e-mail never made it to him, but I received a very nice response from an assistant saying that Mr. Lloyd would be happy to lead our group around the garden for a measly fee of £1,500! That was way beyond our group's budget, but fortunately I was able to secure Fergus Garrett, head gardener of Great Dixter, for a more reasonable price.

Fergus Garrett is funny and knowledgeable and the tour was outstanding. After Fergus left us, there was time for everyone to revisit areas of the garden at their leisure. We were just starting to disperse when one of the women on the tour ran up to tell me that she had seen Christopher Lloyd out in the garden with a photographer. I asked everyone to stay put a minute, and I ran to find him in hopes of engaging him in a conversation.

When I found him, I walked right up and said, "Dan Hinkley says you're a wild man." He harrumphed and stammered, but then started to laugh. We started to talk about Dan and the Pacific Northwest and, slowly but surely, all of the people on my tour came over to meet him. Very quickly the conversation turned to gardening, and before long Christopher Lloyd was leading us around showing us his favorite plants and telling fascinating stories.

It just goes to show that even the world's most famous gardeners can't resist talking gardening with an enthusiastic group. When we loaded back on the bus, everyone was buzzing with excitement about getting to meet the famous owner of Great Dixter. Christopher Lloyd passed away in 2006, but I'll always have fond memories of touring the garden with him, and I still remember his wave good-bye as he stood in front of his house with his wiener dog by his side.

Something similar happened when I brought a group to see Beth Chatto's equally famous garden near Colchester, England. Beth Chatto is the author of several bestselling books about her garden, known for its wide range of habitats: everything from desert-dry gravelly soil to stream-fed bog. Once again, her fee for a garden tour was beyond our budget, but she very kindly agreed to greet us and give us a brief introduction to the garden for a reasonable price.

She was just finishing the introduction when practically every woman on the tour began complimenting her pants. She was wearing really cool pants obviously made for gardening. They had lots of pockets and places for tools but they were also quite fashionable. Soon the women and Beth Chatto were engaged in a lively discussion about garden clothes. That somehow led to a discussion about favorite garden tools, and because the enthusiasm of our group was so infectious, she began describing her favorite plants and soon she was leading us around the garden to show them to us. Before I realized it, well over ninety minutes had gone by, and Beth Chatto had just led our group on a tour of her entire garden. She died in May 2018, and I'll always consider myself lucky to have met such a kind and knowledgeable person, not to mention touring her wonderful garden with her.

Of all the famous gardeners I've met on my tours, one I'll never forget is the Norwegian Princess Greta Sturdza. She created Le Vasterival in Normandy, France, by transforming 30 acres of wild thicket into a magical English-style garden filled with color, scent, and rare plants. The princess herself led all of the tours of her garden. When I brought a group there in 2002, she was in her eighties but spry as a twenty-year-old.

Before the tour started, the princess stood on a stump to go over the rules of the garden. She held a long-handled, three-pronged weeding tool in her hand as she recited the dos and don'ts of the garden. She came across so stern and serious, I began to worry about what kind of tour we were in for.

Her first rule was that picture taking was not allowed. If you wanted pictures or slides of the garden, you had to buy them in the gift shop. The second rule was that wandering alone on your own in the garden was not allowed. You had to stay with the group. Rule number three was to use the toilet before the tour began. You were not allowed to use it again until the tour was over.

Then the princess asked us if we were wondering why she was holding the weeding tool in her hand. She said that the first time she saw one of us step into any of her garden beds, she would give a warning. Then she waved the weeding tool menacingly and said, "The second time I see you step in one of my garden beds, you get this!" We all laughed and the princess led us out into the garden for the tour.

The tour was fantastic. The princess knew her plants and was a great guide to boot. She gave useful garden tips and introduced us to all sorts of rare and unusual plants. One spectacular tree she showed us has become one of my all-time favorites. The wedding-cake tree (*Cornus controversa* 'Variegata') is a rare and elegant tree featuring horizontal branches that grow in layers similar to those on a wedding cake. The leaves are bordered in creamy white, and attractive white flowers grace the spreading branches in May. In late summer, glistening black berries, highly attractive to birds, are carried above the variegated leaves. This tree requires well-drained soil in an open area in light shade and will burn in full sun. It eventually can reach 35 feet tall and wide, so make sure there's room for its tiered branches to spread. Heed the princess's warning that any pruning on this tree will ruin its gorgeous form.

The tour had been going for about a half hour when a shocking surprise occurred. The princess goosed me with her weeding tool! I screamed and jumped at least 3 feet in the air. I know for sure I never stepped into any of her garden beds, and she definitely didn't give me a warning. The only person laughing harder than everyone on the tour was the princess herself.

I don't know if she did this to all of the tour leaders when groups visited her garden, but I suspect she might well have. Even I had to laugh when she gave me a mischievous wink when no one was looking. I enjoyed the rest of the tour, but I definitely kept a close eye on the princess until I was safely back on the bus! Princess Greta Sturdza died in November 2009, but she'll definitely live in the memory of everyone who witnessed her naughty side on that tour.

Garden Shows Are Full of Surprises

I have led two garden tours of England, both in spring so we could include a visit to the Chelsea Flower Show. Run by the Royal Horticultural Society, it takes place in May on the grounds of the Royal Hospital Chelsea in London. The heart of the show is the magnificent display gardens. They're created by some of the world's most famous garden designers, who pull out all the stops in their bid to win an RHS gold medal and the coveted award for best show garden. Each garden takes months of planning, features innovative design ideas, and contains all varieties of structures, stone walls, hardscape, fences, new plant introductions, incredible blooming plant combinations, garden art, and more.

Of course, there is much more to experience than the display gardens at the Chelsea Flower Show. There are incredible plant exhibits put together by some of England's most famous nurseries. The displays are filled with every kind of plant imaginable, including rare and unusual ones from far-flung corners of the globe. One display that stands out in my memory included every known variety of delphinium, with every plant in full bloom. Many of the vendors are nursery owners who are world-famous gardeners in their own right.

One year I had the good fortune to meet and talk to the late David Austin, founder of David Austin Roses. He was the first person to successfully cross modern English roses with old-fashioned ones in order to produce repeat-blooming roses with old-fashioned rose fragrance. Mr. Austin was very friendly and had a story about every one of the many hybrids he had produced, all of which were blooming away in his flower display.

The shopping at the Chelsea show is to die for. You'll find a host of exhibitors selling innovative and must-have horticultural products. There is incredible garden art for sale as well. I paid about £60 for *Wally*, my adorable little bronze snail. Not only is he a wonderful souvenir of our visit to Chelsea, but to this day, he remains one of my favorite works of garden art. The artist who created *Wally* also had larger sculptures that sold for thousands of pounds, but alas, they were beyond my budget. If all of the shopping and garden viewing tires you out, buy lunch at one of the many food vendors and squeeze into an open spot on the lawn to picnic while enjoying live music from the centrally located gazebo.

If you decide to go to the show, I strongly recommend joining the Royal Horticultural Society for a year. With membership you are eligible for discounted entry to any RHS show, receive a monthly subscription to *The Garden* (one of my favorite gardening magazines), and get reduced entry fees to most of the famous gardens in England, plus it allows you to visit the Chelsea show on members-only day when the show is purported to be much less crowded. On our garden tours to England, we bought everyone on the tour a membership so we could visit the show on the less-crowded day.

The first time we visited Chelsea with a group was in 2000, the year the show made a major change. Previously it had been held in big temporary tents, but that year it was held in the newly constructed Great Pavilion, a very large permanent structure. Overcrowding has always been a problem at the show, and despite the fact that we were there on members-only day, the show was jam-packed. All you could do was inch along with the crowd as it worked its way past displays. I was stuck next to a very nice English woman and before long we struck up a conversation.

I knew that English people love tradition, and I'd heard that there had been grumbling about the new pavilion in place of the tents, so I asked my new acquaintance how she felt about it. She said she was delighted with the change because the show wasn't nearly as crowded as it used to be!

Many of the people that came on our first England tour were excited to travel again, and France seemed to be the next country of interest. My wife, Mary, and I had been to France many times, but never with a focus on gardens. Therefore we took on the difficult task of scouting out gardens in France in September 2001. Besides gardens, we decided another show like Chelsea would be great fun and found the International Garden Festival at the Domaine de Chaumont-sur-Loire in France, also known as the French garden show. The show is totally different from Chelsea. There is minimal shopping and there are no nursery displays. Instead, the outdoor festival is all about the show gardens. It remains open from April through November and the gardens evolve during the six months they are on display.

Mary and I absolutely loved the French garden show. It's held on the estate of Chaumont-sur-Loire Château, with the beautiful late-tenth-century castle as a backdrop. Every year, about thirty artists and landscape design teams are chosen from hundreds of conceptual submissions to create contemporary gardens on a specific theme.

The year we went to check it out, the theme was Mosaïculture. It's the French word for the Victorian tradition of bedding out, where plants are arranged to look like the intricate patterns of a carpet. The gardens were beautiful, interesting, and thought-provoking. One memorable garden contained big colorful topiaries of birds taking off in flight, while another more whimsical garden featured bowling balls painted to look like heads rising above a sea of ornamental grasses. The gardens are designed to challenge notions about landscape design and life in general. It's great fun to explore the garden before reading the written description that explains the concept each garden is meant to convey.

We were excited to include the French garden show on the tour we were to lead the following spring. I had told the tour participants about it and they were excited as well. But I'll never forget the surprised looks on everyone's faces when we walked into the show to be greeted by the sight of the two biggest boobs on earth! They were right in the center of the garden show and were bright pink, at least 20 feet tall and almost as wide. Unbeknownst to us, the theme for that year's garden show was Eroticism in the Garden. This could only happen in France.

As it turned out, the gardens were a bit wild, but very fun and colorful. We had a great tour of the gardens by a knowledgeable horticulturist, and everyone ended up loving the show.

The following spring, I gave a seminar about the gardens of France at the Northwest Flower and Garden show in Seattle. Of course, I included the French garden show in my talk, and I couldn't resist shocking the tweetle out of the audience by showing a slide of the giant boobs. Wouldn't you know that was the one slide in the entire talk that got stuck in the projector? It took what seemed like forever for the audiovisual person to get it free.

Imagine what it was like, trying to kill five minutes of dead time in front of an audience with nothing to look at but two giant boobs on the big screen!

The Adventures Continue

One of the best things about travel (and life) is when experiences that begin as disasters end up as the best stories. My favorites are those situations where creative solutions save the day. That's what happened when my wife, Mary, and I accompanied a garden group to southern France and northern Italy. The plan was to fly to Nice from Seattle via London; meet Brad, our travel organizer, at the Nice airport; then take a two-hour bus ride to our hotel where we would enjoy a welcome dinner together. Since the plane wasn't scheduled to land until after six in the evening, the dinner at the hotel was planned for around nine that night.

The tour got off to a difficult start. As the 747 was taxiing on the Seattle runway, one of the people on our tour noticed that fluid was pouring out of one of the wings. The plane had to turn around for repairs, and we ended up taking off three hours late. OK, he probably saved all our lives, but I'm still upset with him for looking out the window and delaying the flight.

I was worried the whole flight to London because I knew we would miss our connection to Nice. Luckily, when we arrived the British Airways staff was waiting for us, and they transferred the whole group onto a flight that would leave soon. We landed in Nice shortly after nine o'clock. Brad was relieved to see us, and we all went out to load onto the tour bus, giddy with excitement.

When the bus driver turned the key in the ignition, nothing happened, not even a sputter. He tried a few more times but it was futile. I figured that the bus driver would call for assistance and we would soon be on our way, but to my dismay, he said the bus company would send another bus as a replacement. He wasn't sure how long it would take, but it sounded like we were in for a long wait. At first everyone took it well, but after an hour went by, we were all getting quite restless. A gloom descended on our giddiness as we sat helplessly on the bus, tired and hungry.

That's when someone in our group came up with the idea of pushing the bus to allow the driver to pop the clutch to see if it would start. I asked the driver if we could try it, but he was hesitant. It was a large bus and he was worried about liability if anyone got hurt. Furthermore, the bus was parked on flat ground, and he didn't believe we'd be able to get it to move, let alone build up enough speed for the clutch method to start the engine. I kept working on the driver and he finally agreed to try it. All twenty-three of us on the tour got behind the bus. There wasn't room for everyone to push the bus, so we made a chain with the biggest, strongest people actually pushing the bus and the rest of us pushing them.

At first it seemed hopeless. The bus just wouldn't budge. Then it started rocking back and forth. Everyone pushed harder, and the big bus slowly began rolling forward. That fired us up and we all pushed harder. The bus started picking up speed. Someone yelled "Go for it" and the driver popped the clutch. The engine sputtered, smoke came out of the exhaust, and suddenly the bus roared to life. Everyone started to cheer, while I shouted at the top of my lungs, "Get on the bus. Let's go before it quits again!"

Thank goodness it kept running, and we finally pulled into our hotel at two in the morning. We had called ahead to let the hotel know our arrival time, and to my amazement, they had a huge spread waiting for us. All of the pent-up excitement led to quite a raucous party on the hotel patio. I suspect most of the hotel patrons didn't get much sleep that night, but instead of treating us like ugly Americans, most of the hotel guests laughed about it. There's something special about seeing a group of travelers having fun!

Incidentally, that tour ended up being one of the best ever. The weather was perfect, the scenery along the Côte d'Azur and the Italian lakes region was to die for, and we visited some of the most beautiful gardens in the world. We even caught a glimpse of Paul Allen's yacht. It was twice the size of any other boat floating in the bay.

In case you're wondering, I'm not retiring or slowing down. Mary and I just returned from a midwinter trip to the Lemon Festival in France, and we're hosting a garden tour to Japan in the fall. People who frequent our tours are already suggesting future destinations, so I expect to lead many more tours and experience plenty of new travel adventures. I continue to host my Saturday radio show on KIRO 97.3 FM and make regular appearances on *New Day NW* and *Take 5* on KING 5 TV. And I'm already booked solid for garden talks well into next year.

I've certainly never lost my love for gardening. My goal is to have the best garden in Seattle—or at least make my side better than Mary's. Nothing makes me happier than being out in my overcrowded garden with my pups at my side, walking around trying to figure out where in the world to plant my newest rare treasure.

Speaking of pooches, we've had quite a few of them over the years. In fact, Mary and I measure how long we've been married by how many four-footed kids we've had. The newest addition to our family is Izzy, part black Lab, part border collie, and part golden retriever—and, judging by the sound of her bark, part beagle. She was a puppy rescue. We had three pups to choose from: the big one, the calm one, or the really active one. What was I thinking when I chose the really active one! Just over a year old now, she has bitten holes in the walls of our house, destroyed our couches, chewed up the rug, eaten my hearing aid, and still beats the living tweetle out of any plant she can gain access to. But other than that, she's the sweetest, cuddliest dog we've ever had. I can't wait to see what happens when we adopt a little brother for her!

Oh, and don't think for one moment this is going to be my last book. As the saying goes, "No rest for the wicked." I already have an idea for the next one. Oh, la la: I can't wait to get started!

Index

About the Author

Ciscoe Morris loves gardening and storytelling. He is a horticultur-ist and popular TV and radio host. He wrote a weekly newspaper column for seventeen years, first for the *Seattle Post-Intelligencer*, followed by the *Seattle Times*. His latest book, *Ask Ciscoe*, was among the top-selling garden books nationwide. Ciscoe spent the majority of his long gardening career as director of grounds care at Seattle University, where he developed a nationally recognized organic gardening program. Additionally, he has been a longtime master gardener, an International Society of Arboriculture certified arborist, and a Washington State Nursery & Landscape Association certified professional horticulturist. When he isn't off speaking at events throughout the Pacific Northwest and beyond, you'll find him working in his northeast Seattle garden, which has been fea-tured in several publications. Besides gardening, he is passionate about travel. Despite his busy schedule, he manages to find time to host garden tours all over the world.